LastPass Guide

Make your passwords wicked strong

Benjamin Bryan

Questions, Comments, and Christmas Cards can be
sent to:

B3N LLC
PO Box 238
Ponderey, ID 83852

ben@b3n.org

Library of Congress Control Number: 2021905250

ISBN: 978-1-955199-00-1 (Paperback)

ISBN: 978-1-955199-01-8 (eBook)

This book can also be purchased as a PDF at:
https://b3n.org/lastpass-guide

Subscribe to my tech newsletter at:
https://b3n.org/subscribe

Manuscript Version: 2021-03-20.

Free Download – 10 Steps to Securing Windows 10

Anyone reading this book may get my <u>10 Step Guide to Securing Windows 10</u> at no cost.

<u>https://b3n.org/freedownload</u>

Table of Contents

Chapter 1: Ahoy!

I would guess you try your best to pick good passwords. Perhaps you're making sure to use a mix of uppercase, lowercase, numbers, and special characters that you can remember. Whether you're writing them down in a paper notebook (that might get lost), or memorizing them you've probably got passwords for hundreds of accounts: Google, Office365, Evernote, Facebook, Twitter, Amazon, Netflix, LinkedIn, Ebay, PayPal, GitHub, American Express, Vanguard, Wells Fargo, Chipotle, Minecraft, Uber, Delta, Trello, Discover, Etsy, L.L. Bean, Slack, Staples, Costco, Wal-Mart, Home Depot, Lowes, Southern California Edison, Wall Street Journal ...

I bet you have more than a hundred accounts. In fact, if you start counting all your accounts, **you probably have around a billion logins** at various websites. And you're supposed to have a unique password for each one! Good luck with that! If you're not writing every password down on post-it notes stored under your keyboard (which is totally secure) and you're trying to memorize all those passwords it is highly probable that you are using the same password for almost all your sites! That's bad.

But first, writing all your passwords down in a notebook (that you might lose on a trip for someone else to find) isn't a best practice, and memorizing a billion passwords is unsustainable. If you are memorizing that many passwords it likely means your passwords are weak, old man.

For years I struggled with coming up with unique passwords. I came up with what I thought was a pretty good solution where I had made up one extremely difficult to memorize password and then I'd append the first 2 letters of the website to the end to make it unique. But this failed because **websites have inconsistent password requirements.** Some require a special character and an uppercase, some prohibit it, some require more than 12 characters, some won't allow more than 8! Some sites force a password reset every 90 days and won't allow re-using a password! It ended up being impossible to memorize every exception and rule for every site! And I'm not a casual computer user, I've been in the technology field for 20 years. If I struggle with this, surely everyone else is! About 8 years ago I discovered password managers, and that completely changed how I manage passwords. Now all of my passwords are strong. Wicked Strong!

Here are some reactions I've received after generating passwords:

- "Uh …nobody is going to crack your password. Ever."
- "I'm just going to bang my head against a wall."
- "You are insane!"
- "Dude. I can't type that."
- "Do not let Ben pick the admin password!"
- "Wicked Strong!"

Why am I getting responses like that? My passwords look like this:

c92IniL%1b!&5GCnpHyyer

49RjT$5qYeksIvM6jXmYP^

1Qh9@$gpJq3b#8IkhohC3y

BenIsAwesome!123*

Every one of my accounts has a distinct password and they all look something like one of the above

---

* Sarcasm

passwords. My coworkers think I'm a genius for memorizing unique complex passwords for a billion sites. I'd like to tell them I'm a genius with a photographic memory and have all my passwords memorized. But I don't. What's my secret? I only memorize one password[†]. And that is why I'm writing this. So that you can have strong passwords like me, and to do so **you only need to memorize one password.**

The one password you need to memorize is your LastPass password. It is the master key to unlock all others. Make it a good hard password that you've never used and never will use anywhere else. Don't forget it and that's the last password you will ever need.

Now imagine you could use that one password, the only one you need to remember, and use that to unlock any of your sensitive information whenever, and wherever you happen to be anywhere in the world, or even in outer-space (in case you are on the International Space Station or a sight-seeing trip to VY Canis Majoris). Everything from social media

---

[†] So, after thinking about this I really memorize more than one password… obviously I must know my computer's password so I can login before I can even access LastPass. But the point is I have only a handful of passwords memorized, not a billion.

accounts to bank pin numbers. Encrypted securely, all of it. You can organize the passwords into folders, you can share certain passwords with family or friends. You don't need to be concerned about losing your paper notebook, or your accounts getting hacked due to poor or reused passwords. You don't need to be concerned about forgetting your passwords. It's all there in LastPass. Every password you've ever had or ever will need. Available from your computer or your phone. Secured so that nobody else can see it. **Not even LastPass employees can see** it because it's encrypted with your master password which only you know. If a LastPass employee tries to access your sensitive data, he can't because it's encrypted.‡

Since you're reading this you are likely interested in learning about LastPass. LastPass is the best password manager for the majority of people. LastPass is secure, robust, affordable, and it works with almost all phone and computer platforms in existence (Windows, Linux, Mac OSX, Android, iPhone, Chromebook, etc.). I'm not writing about something I don't use. You'll be happy to know I eat my own dogfood. I use LastPass daily.

---

‡ See Appendix G: Is Some Vault Data Unencrypted to learn about what data is encrypted.

All my logins and passwords are stored in LastPass. Website passwords, database accounts, server logins, bank pins, credit cards, health insurance cards, airline rewards numbers, etc.

My goal in writing this guide is that you will learn to securely manage passwords and it will become as automatic as breathing. You'll just do it without thinking about it.

Let's start with a Glossary, this is mostly because my main inspiration for creating this guide was reading Brett Kelly's Evernote Essentials (which is a great read if you want to get your life organized) and that manual started with his patent pending Glossary (Brett, please don't sue me). So, here's a glossary of terms you'll see throughout this guide:

- ✓ **Vault** – a secure place to store sensitive data like passwords. The vault is secured with a master password.
- ✓ **Items**
  - o **Password** – An Item which stores a password for a website associated to a URL (LastPass should have named this item a Website instead of Password).
  - o **Secure Note** (or Note) – A generic notepad type note that can store anything sensitive.

- Address – Store an identity with an address, phone, birthday, gender, etc. which can be used to auto-populate forms when signing up for accounts or having stuff shipped to you.
- Payment Card – Credit Card information
- Bank Account – Bank information (including PIN, account number, routing and IBAN numbers, etc.)
- Driver's License – Information about your Driver's License
- Membership – Store all your airline reward numbers, gym memberships, etc.
- SSH Key – encryption keys to authenticate against servers
- Passport – this is a passport obviously
- Social Security Number – obvious again
- Insurance Policy – I'm just going to stop explaining these…
- Health Insurance
- Wi-Fi Password
- Email Account
- Instant Messenger
- Database
- Server
- Software License

- o **Custom Types** – create custom item types with your own set of fields.
- ✓ **Security Challenge** – LastPass can use this to analyze all your accounts. It discovers accounts using services that have been compromised, weak, reused, or old passwords.
- ✓ **Sharing Center** – A place to share passwords with others or view a list of passwords shared with you.
- ✓ **Emergency Access** – A way that you can give a trusted family or friend access to your account in case of your death after a specified waiting period.
- ✓ **Family Members** – Family members in your household that you share a password folder with.
- ✓ **Master Password** – A password that is used to secure all your other passwords.
- ✓ **Multifactor Authentication** – another layer of account protection – in order to login to an account both a password and some other form of authentication (such as Google Authenticator) must be used to access the account. Multifactor Authentication (MFA) is also commonly referred to as Two Factor Authentication (2FA).
- ✓ **Trusted Device** – When multifactor authentication is enabled a trusted device only needs a 2nd factor every 30 days.

- ✓ **Never URLs** – URLs where you don't want LastPass to autofill or remember passwords (this is rarely needed for problematic sites—I have come across a total of 1 website that doesn't work well with LastPass out of a billion).
- ✓ **Equivalent Domains** – A list of domains that share the same login information. E.g. YouTube.com, Gmail.com, Google.com all share the same credentials so LastPass will treat them as equivalent instead of creating a separate Password Item for each site.
- ✓ **One-time passwords** – Passwords that can only be used once. Useful if you need to access LastPass from an untrusted device (which you should never ever do. Don't use this feature to login on untrusted devices).
- ✓ **History** – A history of previous passwords for an Item.
- ✓ **Identity** – An identity within LastPass. Essentially it allows you to divide your vault into sub-vaults (such as 'Home' or 'Work') so that you can only see passwords related to that identity.

Chapter 2: Pricing

What does LastPass cost? The basic LastPass plan is Free. It is missing a few features found in the paid versions so I would generally recommend upgrading to one of the paid plans (you can always start out with the free plan).

How much do the plans cost?

For 1 person, LastPass Premium is $3/month. Or the Families plan is $4/month for the whole family which gives up to 6 of your family members access to LastPass Premium (and a few extra sharing features for families) and is a fantastic deal. For Small Businesses look at LastPass Teams ($4/month per user) and for larger businesses look at LastPass Enterprise ($6/month per user).

Feature/Plan	Free	Premium	Families	Teams	Enterprise
Monthly	$0	$3	$4	$4/user	$6/user
Users	1	1	6	5 to 50	5+
Both Desktop and Mobile	✗	✓	✓	✓	✓
Vault	✓	✓	✓	✓	✓
One to One Sharing	✓	✓	✓	✓	✓
Multi-factor Auth	✓	✓	✓	✓	✓
LastPass Authenticator	✓	✓	✓	✓	✓
Emergency Access	✗	✓	✓	✗	✗
Advanced Multifactor Options	✗	✓	✓	✓	✓
Priority Support	✗	✓	✓	✓	✓
LastPass for Applications	✗	✓	✓	✓	✓
1GB encrypted file storage	✗	✓	✓	✓	✓
6 Premium Licenses	✗	✗	✓	✗	✗
Family manager dashboard	✗	✗	✓	✗	✗
Unlimited Shared Folders	✗	✗	✓	✓	✓
Directory Integration	✗	✗	✗	✓	✓
Single Sign-On	✗	✗	✗	✗	✓
Standard Policies	✗	✗	✗	✓	✓
Advanced Policies	✗	✗	✗	✗	✓

I know some people and businesses will balk at the price. But it is worth the cost. Just some of the benefits you get with a **Premium, Families, Team, or Enterprise plan**:

1. **Use on both Desktop and Mobile Devices.** The free plan on LastPass forces you to choose a device type. You can choose Desktop devices, or Mobile devices. With a paid plan you are allowed to use both device types.

2. **Shared Password Folders.** You can create shared password folders for your family (handy for sharing Netflix, Amazon Prime Video, Hulu, or whatever sites you all are using these days) as well as sensitive documents like Driver's License numbers. You can also fine-tune access by only allowing your kids to have access to certain passwords while your husband can see everything. And your individual passwords can still be kept separate.

3. **One to many Sharing.** I have found a lot of businesses use LastPass, from small home office businesses to Fortune 500 companies. So, when I need to share credentials to a client or vendor chances are they use LastPass so it's nice to simply share a password instead of trying to find some other way to send it to them securely.

4. **Emergency Access.** This is one of my favorite features and a great way to make things easier for your loved ones in case of your death. You can add any LastPass user as a trusted Emergency Access Contact. You can add anyone you want: your

wife, your kids, a trusted friend. This feature allows you to ensure your family has access to your accounts in the event of your death or incapacitation. <u>But not before.</u> The way this works is anyone in your Emergency Access trusted list can request access to your passwords. You can set up a waiting period between immediately and 30 days. LastPass will send you an email telling you they have requested emergency access to your passwords, and then you have a chance to deny it during the waiting period.

5. **Advanced Multifactor Factor Authentication** – an extra security step required to gain access to your passwords. Premium allows for more options such as YubiKey hardware authenticators.

6. **1GB of encrypted file storage** – upload images of important documents like your Passport, Driver's License, and Birth Certificate all stored encrypted just in case you need it (or lose it while traveling).

7. **LastPass for Applications** – I don't use this, but it can auto-fill desktop applications (e.g. Quicken). Honestly LastPass for Applications is more trouble than it's worth.

8. **Priority Tech support** – I have contacted LastPass support once to ask a technical security question, which got escalated up to an engineer who answered my question accurately. That's excellent service.

LastPass will save you time and I believe it's well worth the cost. Figure out what your time is worth by dividing your annual salary into dollars per hour:

[annual salary] / (52 – [weeks of vacation]) / [hours worked per week]

For example:

$50,000 / (52 – 4) / 40 = **$26/hour**

$100,000 / (52 – 2) / 40 = **$50/hour**

(If you don't work but stay at home to take care of the kids a good rule of thumb to find out what your time is worth is to just double your spouse's salary).

So, in the above scenarios if LastPass saves you 1 or 2 hours over a year it more than pays for itself. Now your salary may be less than that or more than that, but I would wager that LastPass will save you much more than 24 hours of productivity over the course of a year in not having to remember or reset forgotten passwords, not having to find a secure way to share a password with a family member, not losing your paper notebook of passwords (that your dog may chew up), not having to stop what you're doing 3 times a day to tell your husband your Amazon Prime or Netflix password again.

A single 5-minute interruption to deal with password issues will get you out of the "zone" and cost you 30-40 minutes to mentally get back to being productive.

If it saves you one extra trip to the bank because you forgot your ATM pin and can just look it up on your phone using the LastPass app instead of driving back home to find your paper password notebook (which could burn up in a house fire) it was worth it.

The price of LastPass is nothing compared to the time it saves.

Chapter 3: Getting Started

A Few More Notes About This Guide

Since I'm using LastPass for Families as I write this guide there may be a few differences if you're using the Free, Premium, or one of the various Business plans. I'll try to point out paid features with a ($). But the concepts in general and usage should remain the same regardless of your plan.

LastPass may change their interface or add more features from time to time. If you are subscribed to my mailing list (by following the free download link on page 3), I'll let you know whenever I release an update.

Also, it should be apparent, but this is not an official guide made by LastPass. This guide takes a different approach than the official documentation which you'll find on LastPass's website.

How to Use This Guide

This guide is meant to be a **step-by-step** guide. It will teach you concepts as you go—and it will make the most sense if you follow along. At the end of each chapter look for **action items**. You will get the most out of this book if you do those action items before moving to the next chapter.

Creating a LastPass Account

Head over to https://www.lastpass.com and click on the "Get LastPass Free" Button (you can't miss it):

Then, obviously, sign up for an account. You'll soon be prompted to create a **Master Password...**

Now We Must Talk About Your Master Password

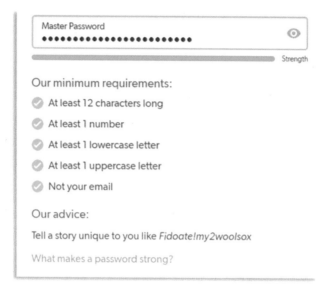

Your Master Password is important. Very important. This password can be used to decrypt all your other passwords and sensitive information stored in LastPass. If your Master Password gets compromised everything in LastPass gets compromised.

Now there are safeguards such as Multifactor Authentication and Country restrictions you should put in place (which I'll cover later) that may protect your account even with a compromised master password. Remember, security comes in layers like

an onion… but **the Master Password is the most important layer** here. It is **YOUR** responsibility to maintain the confidentiality of your password and to pick a unique and secure one.

LastPass has great advice for picking a strong master password: https://blog.lastpass.com/2015/07/how-to-make-a-strong-master-password.html/

If you don't have time to read that, the gist of it is you don't need to come up with a random string of characters that's difficult to remember. Rather come up with a phrase at least 30 characters that is unique to you. Don't pick something based on a common phrase like "To be or not to be that is the question." Pick something weird and unique that you can remember but hackers would have a hard time guessing and mix in some numbers and special characters:

flyingMybulldozer^over4Turtles

EatSomeJellyOnToast[]InSan8Francisco

MyMouseHas300Buttons….AndNoneOfThemWork$

Don't use these. Because I wrote them in this book they're already compromised and added to every password cracking database... but you get the idea.

Make sure you pick a new password that you have never used anywhere else. This one needs to be unique.

After you pick your Master Password (did I mention it needs to be a good one?) do what you need to do to make sure you don't forget it. Make up a song and dance. Write it on a piece of paper temporarily if you must. But once you are sure you won't forget it, start a fire. Take that piece of paper and burn it. Then roast some marshmallows.

Action Items:

- ✓ **Create a LastPass Account**
- ✓ **Pick a Strong Master Password**
- ✓ **Roast Marshmallows**

Chapter 4: Installing

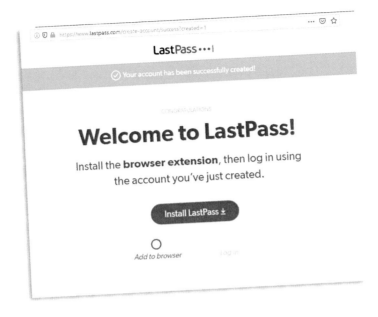

Now, LastPass has a Browser Extension and a Desktop Application ($). Honestly, the Desktop Application isn't very good; I've had lots of trouble with it. Almost everyone uses the LastPass Browser Extension instead. About the only advantage the LastPass Desktop Application has is it can automatically fill in desktop application passwords (such as the Quicken Vault) instead of having to copy/paste from the Browser Extension. If you want this feature go ahead and install it, otherwise stick to the Browser Extension (also there's no reason you can't install both).

There are two versions of the Browser Extensions. The Open Source version or the Binary (aka "Full") version. The Binary version is only available for Chrome, Firefox, Opera, and Safari. The main reason to use the open source version is trust verification. If you are a programmer and want to inspect the code to know that it's trustworthy you can do that. You can verify that it's encrypting your passwords using a strong algorithm before sending them to LastPass's servers.

If you haven't already, go ahead and download and install the LastPass Browser Extension: https://lastpass.com/download/

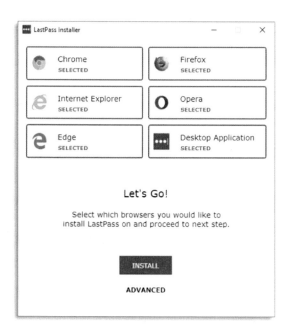

Unless you are paranoid, I suggest installing the binary version. It gives you several minor extra features, but my favorite feature of the binary component is you can upload file attachments ($).

The easiest way to install the binary version of LastPass for all your Browsers is to get the **Universal Installer** for your OS. That will install the Extension for any browser you'd like (or all of them). *By default it will install the binray version which is what most people do. If you don't want binary uncheck that from the "Advanced" settings before installing.*

Logging into the Browser Extension

The LastPass Icon is always top-right of your browser and looks like this:

Or this:

Don't panic when you see the red LastPass icon. In most other situations red means bad. If I'm looking at the dash on my car for example: green means good to go, yellow means warning—better have someone look at the car soon, and red means the engine is about to explode. But in LastPass red is not bad.

Red means logged in. Grey means not logged in. You may also see Yellow which means you're logged in but LastPass has detected a problem such as you have a duplicate password…but we'll deal with that later.

Click the LastPass icon to login. If you're logged in, you can click it and choose "Open my Vault" to view your passwords.

Action Items:

- ✓ **Install LastPass Browser Extension**
- ✓ **Login to LastPass with your Browser Extension**
- ✓ **Open the Vault**

Chapter 5: The Vault

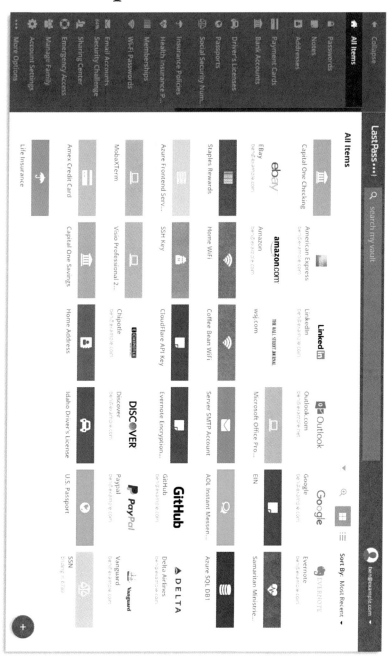

This is what a LastPass Vault looks like. It is a list of all your passwords and encrypted items. I should note that "Vault" is a poor name because not all the info in your Vault is encrypted (See: <u>Appendix G: Is Some Vault Data Unencrypted</u>)

You'll notice that you can see all your Items: Passwords, Notes, Addresses, Payment Cards, etc.

Filter by Item Type

On the left pane you can choose to filter by any Item Type.

If you're looking for **Wi-Fi Passwords** for example, click it (bottom left) and you'll see a list of all your wireless passwords.

Display Options

On the top right you have some display options:

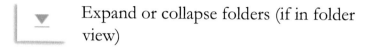 Expand or collapse folders (if in folder view)

Card View (this is my favorite view)

Folder View

Increase or decrease size of Items

 Change the sorting options. I like to leave it sorted by Most Recent which hides folders (I really don't care about folders but some people like them).

Chapter 6: Password Items

Now it's time to create your first password.

To create a new item, if you're in the Vault, hit the plus (**+**) button on the bottom right.

Or hit the LastPass browser extension icon and choose Add Item:

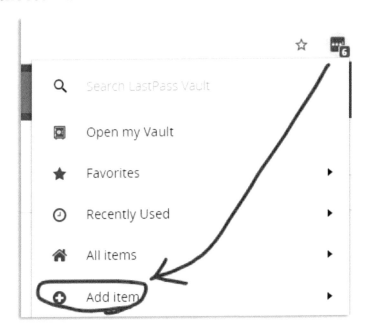

You'll be presented with several Item Types. **The most common item is simply "Password" which LastPass should have named "Website"** …so whenever you see "Password Item" just remember they meant "Website."

Item Types:

Let's take a quick look at a Password Item (top left). All the item types are similar—the main difference is the fields available.

Tip: Always use the proper item types. If you are storing something that is not a website, do not use the "Password" Item type. "Secure Note" is a great generic item type.

First Look at An Item –Password Item (Website)

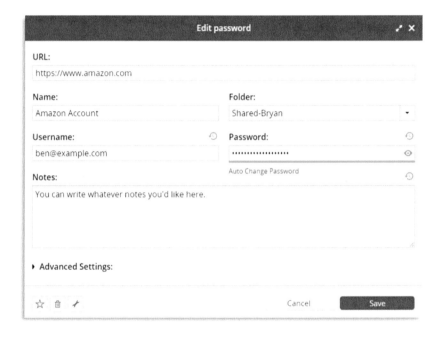

URL: LastPass will match this with the URL in your browser, so if you go to www.amazon.com it will automatically fill out your credentials from this Item.

Name: You can name it anything you want.

Folder: The folder this password is stored in. All Shared folders are prefixed with "Shared-" so you can easily tell that it's shared with others.

Username: Self explanatory

Password: Normally LastPass will automatically fill out the credentials, but if you'd like to view the password hit the eye icon.

Notes: Whatever you want to write here. Sometimes I'll put answers to security questions here so I can remember them later.

 You'll also notice a couple of history buttons. You can click those to view previous versions of your username, password, or notes.

Normally you don't need to go into the advanced stuff, but if you expand **Advanced Settings,** you'll see some additional options:

▾ Advanced Settings:
Require Password Reprompt ☑ Autologin Disable AutoFill

☆ 🗑 ⚲ Cancel Save

Require Password Reprompt: This is for high security items. This requires that you re-enter your Master Password whenever you access this Item. It is <u>annoying</u> so use this feature sparingly. I only enable this on very important and rarely used Password Items.

Autologin: For example, when you visit Amazon.com it will not only automatically fill in your username and password, but also hit the "login" button for you.

Disable AutoFill: Prevents LastPass from automatically filling in your credentials. Instead you must right-click the login box and manually tell LastPass to fill it. This is useful if you have a website that doesn't work well with LastPass and it's filling data fields it shouldn't (very rare) or in the case that you have multiple logins for the same website, but you only want one to auto-fill (you can always override this at the time of login).

Lastly, you'll see 3 or 4 icons:

 The star just adds it to your favorites. Favorites allows for quick access (LastPass icon → Favorites).

You can guess what the Trashcan does. All deleted items will show up in Deleted Items folder for 30 days and can be recovered during that time. After 30 days they are automatically wiped.

The Sharing button only shows up when the Item is not in a Shared-Folder. It allows you to Share this password with individuals (you can share it with any LastPass user, even free users).

Edit Form Fields - The wrench lets you look at the fields that LastPass discovered on the login page and remap them… LastPass works very well with most websites but I have found a couple of poorly designed websites (for example, my small-town utility company) and LastPass had mapped the username to their password field. It was simple enough to fix.

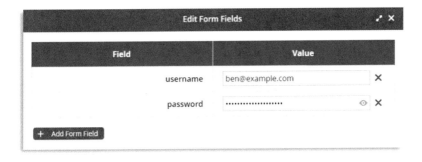

Now let's look at one more Item Type just to demonstrate the difference.

Other Item Types – Health Insurance

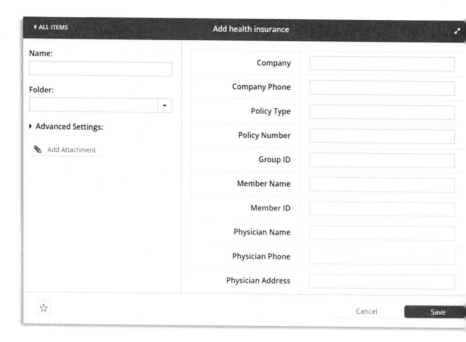

The other item types are similar but have different fields. Here's the Health Insurance item type and you'll notice it's customized for health information. The last field is Notes to add generic information. You can also add a scan of your Health Insurance card as an attachment ($). Now there's one less card you need to keep in your wallet![§]

[§] I still like to keep a hard copy of important cards in my wallet just in case my phone dies. But for things I rarely use and have a low consequence if my phone dies like Airline Memberships, Sears Reward Numbers, etc., those are perfect to put into LastPass so I don't have to carry physical copies everywhere I go.

     LastPass Guide

Tip: If there is no Item Type for the type of secure information you're storing, LastPass has "Secure Notes" which is just like a big encrypted notepad. I use Secure Notes for things like Door Access codes, but you can store whatever you want there. If you need more structure LastPass allows the creation of Custom Item types where you can customize the fields.

Let LastPass Automatically Create New Password Items

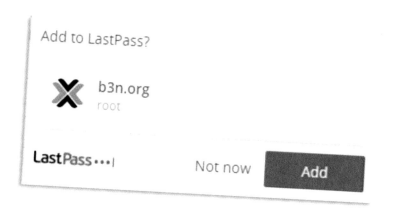

Now, you don't have to go manually creating new Password Items for all your websites… LastPass does it for you automatically. If you are logged into

LastPass (red icon), browse to any website, and whether you login to a website or create a new account, LastPass will capture that data and prompt you to save your username and password as a new Password Item. You'll see an overlay on the top-right of your browser prompting you to add that information to LastPass. Hit "**Add**" and you've saved the password entry.

Similarly, if you change your password on any website, LastPass will detect this and prompt to "**Update**" (picture below).

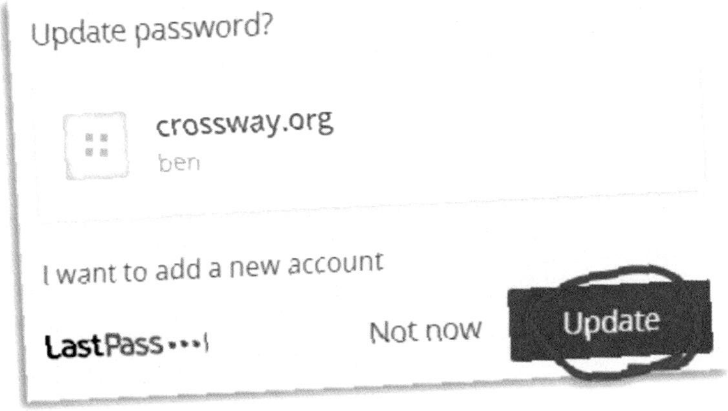

Update password?

crossway.org
ben

I want to add a new account

LastPass ···| Not now   Update

It's as simple as that!

Just by browsing around over the next few months and inevitably logging into all your sites that you'd login to anyway you can eventually get all your website passwords into LastPass.

Generating Secure Passwords

LastPass can generate Secure Random Passwords. When you browse to a website with a change password or new account form, you'll see a lock icon with a circle around it (circled in blue below) on the Password field. Hit that icon which will generate a random password. Click **"Fill Password"**. Simple as that.

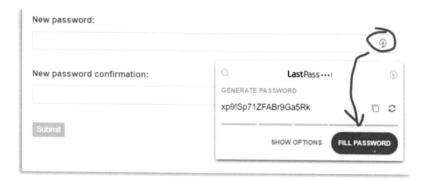

 Tip: On some websites the icon above in the password field won't show up. In that case you can right-click the field, choose LastPass → Generate Secure Password.

LastPass can generate passwords on sites that have restrictions as well:

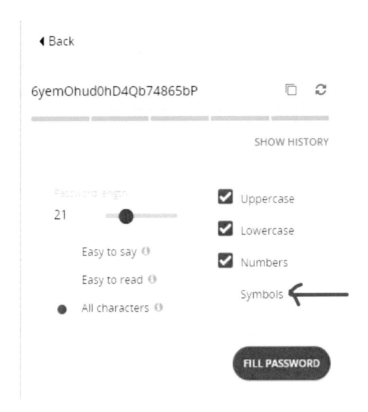

Symbols. Now, you may run across one of those sites that doesn't allow special characters in the password or something ridiculous like that. In that case before you click **"Fill Password"** click **"Show Options"** and now you can unselect symbols.

Likewise, you can also disable **Uppercase**, **Lowercase**, or **Numbers**.

Easy to Say – select this option if you know you'll have to communicate the password audibly to someone. (e.g. a Guest Wireless Password).

Easy to Read – Select this option if you have a password that you will need to type in manually (rarely needed, but sometimes it is)—this feature allows you to avoid characters that look alike such as l and 1 or 0 and o so there's less chance to mistype your password.

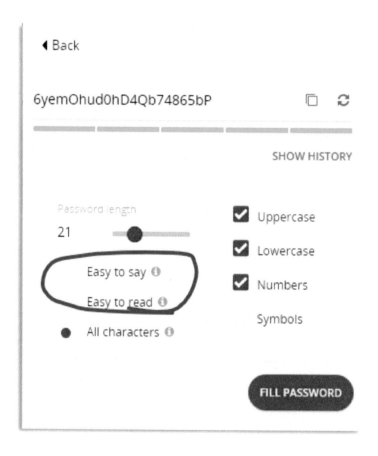

It's most secure to leave it on **All Characters**, so leave it there unless you have a specific case where that doesn't work.

 Tip: The random password generator is your friend. We humans are predictable creatures. It is difficult for us to make up unguessable passwords. It is best to let the LastPass random password generator do it for you for every website. I even have LastPass generate 4-digit PIN codes.

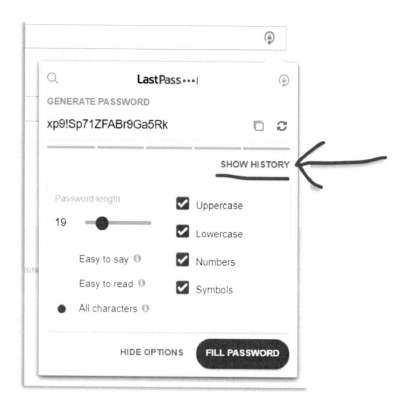

Also, I should note that LastPass keeps a short history of recently generated passwords. If you use LastPass to generate a password and for some reason it doesn't save, you can hit that "SHOW HISTORY" link to view recently generated passwords. I've used this a number of times when LastPass doesn't save the password I generated (this usually only happens on poorly designed websites so it's rare).

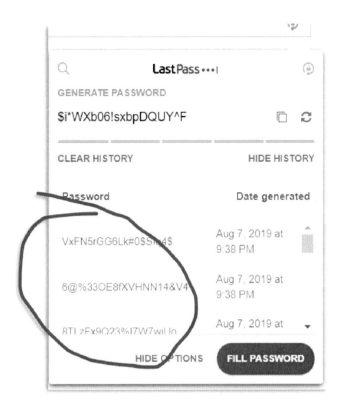

Action Items:

- ✓ **Add a LastPass Password Item**
- ✓ **Add a non-Password Item (e.g. Health Insurance)**
- ✓ **Generate a Secure Password using LastPass**

A Note About Folders

To create a folder hover over the (+) button and choose **"Add New Folder"**

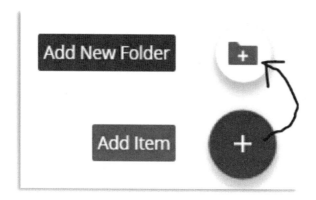

If you're the organized type of person you will be happy to know you can create a hierarchy by adding folders as subfolders. Below I created Folder D under Folder C under Folder B under Folder A.

You can view your items by Folder... LastPass creates its own folders based on the category it thinks the website is and places it there. I am not an organized person, so I don't really use Folders; I think they're a waste of time. But if you like to be organized and want to waste your time feel free to create folders and organize things all you want. To move an item from one folder to another just drag and drop. About the only time I pay attention to folders is when using Shared Folders.

The main reason I don't use Folders is the Search is good. I just type in the site I want, and LastPass finds it. Who needs folders?

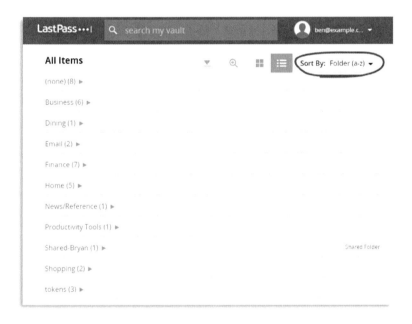

Action Items:

- ✓ **Open your LastPass Vault**
- ✓ **Try changing a few options (Grid View, List View, Sort by...)**
- ✓ **Create a folder**
- ✓ **Move some Items between folders if you so desire**

Chapter 7: Disabling Your Browser's Built-In Password Autofill

Before you get too far you will want to disable your browser's password autofill (often these are not secure) so it's not competing with LastPass to remember passwords. Here's how to do it in a few popular browsers:

Disable Chrome's Built-In Password Manager

Hit the Chrome Menu Toolbar (3 vertical dots)   ⋮

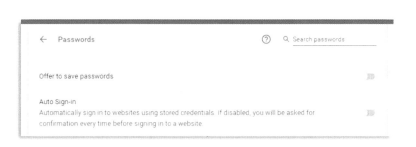

Settings → AutoFill → Passwords → Turn off **"Offer to save passwords"** and **"Auto Sign-in"**.

Settings → AutoFill → Payment Methods → Turn off **"Save and fill payment methods."**

Settings → AutoFill → Address and More → Turn off **"Save and fill addresses"**

Disable Firefox's Built-In Password Manager

Hit the Firefox 3 Horizontal Lines Menu: ≡

Logins and Passwords

☐ Ask to save logins and passwords for websites   Exceptions...

                                                          Saved Logins...

☐ Use a master password   Change Master Password...

Forms and Autofill

☐ Autofill addresses   Learn more   Saved Addresses...

Options → Privacy & Security → Logins and Passwords → Uncheck **"Ask to save logins and passwords for websites"**

Options → Privacy & Security → Forms and Autofill → Uncheck **"Autofill addresses"**

Disable Edge's Built-In Password Manager

Hit Edge's Menu (3 | ... | horizontal dots):

Settings → Your Profile → Passwords → Switch off **"Offer to save passwords"**.

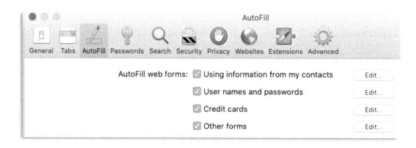

Disable Safari's Built-In Password Manager

Safari Menu → Preferences… → AutoFill → Uncheck **"User names and passwords"** and **"Credit cards."**

Disable Brave's Built-In Password Manager

Hit the 3 horizontal bars in the top-right of Brave →
Settings → Additional Settings (on the left) →
AutoFill → and Uncheck **Passwords, Payment
Methods**, and **Addresses**.

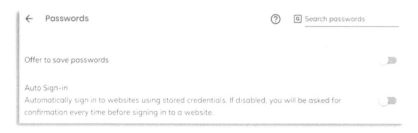

Action Item:

    ✓ **Disable your Browser's built-in password
       Auto-fill**

Chapter 8: Form Fills

Use form fields to quickly fill out websites. LastPass will fill forms for **Payment Cards**, **Bank Accounts**, or **Addresses**. Whether it's providing your Billing and Shipping Address, setting up an ACH transfer, or entering Credit Card info, LastPass can automatically fill any of that information.

I have entered all the addresses I frequently ship to as well as my credit card info into LastPass. This saves a ton of time on checkout pages when ordering online, and one huge advantage is I don't have to be careful about typos.

Create a Form Fill Item

Big Red **"(+)"** → **"Add Item"** → **"Address"** (you could also do Payment Card or Bank Account).

Fill out all the fields you want filled out for you on a form... having shipping address info is useful.

Use a Form Fill

Now, browse to a website where you'd like to fill in that shipping information, such as the Amazon checkout page.

Right-click on the top field → LastPass → Other → choose the Item you'd like to fill in → Fill. LastPass does a pretty good job at automatically filling out all the fields from your Item.

Action Items:

- ✓ **Create Form Fill Items for Payment Cards and Addresses**
- ✓ **Use LastPass to fill out that information on a website**

Chapter 9: Account Settings

On the bottom left of your Vault, click Account Settings.

General

You'll start out on the General tab.

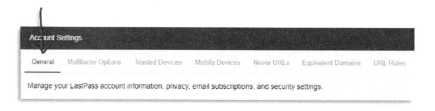

Login Credentials

Here you can change your Email or change your Master Password.

Account Information

Here you can access your account information, payment history, email subscriptions, change your Language, or set your TimeZone

SMS (Text) Account Recovery

Then there's this little option about SMS Account Recovery...

Recovery Phone

This is a way to recover your account via SMS if you forgot your Master Password.

The Problem with SMS. Okay, so most people know that SMS (Short Message Service) aka Texting is not secure. If you don't, you're about to learn why. You could call up my cell phone provider and impersonate me rather easily. You can just tell them you are "Benjamin Bryan". To verify my identity, they may ask you information that's available to the general public just by doing a Google search on my name. They will believe you are me. You tell them "I" got a new SIM card. A few minutes later you pop it in your phone and now you've got access to send and receive texts as "Benjamin Bryan" (please don't try to do this to me, it's rather inconvenient... seriously). For this reason, as a general rule I do not use SMS as a second factor. There is one exception: Google Voice. Google has no customer service so hackers can't con Google into swapping a SIM.

Honestly, I would have told you to never use this feature from LastPass until I looked into it for the purpose of writing this handbook. LastPass has managed to do this securely.

If you turn this feature on, here's what happens. Every time you login to the LastPass Extension on a computer (not a phone) LastPass will generate an OTP (One Time Password) on your local computer.

LastPass doesn't have access to this OTP and a different one is stored for each browser and each computer that you use.

 If you forget your Master Password, LastPass will send an SMS with a code to your phone, you'll enter that code into LastPass on a computer you have logged into LastPass before and this unlocks the OTP code which can decrypt your vault and you can then use that to start the account recovery process.

How safe is this?

In order to compromise your account, **a hacker would need access to receive texts** sent to your phone (which as I mentioned above is easy) and **also have access to a computer where you have previously logged into LastPass.** That should not be so easy. Chances are if they have access to a computer you've logged into LastPass they would have other means to gain access to your account. You should never login to LastPass on a computer that you don't own and control. See Always maintain Physical Possession of Your Devices in

Appendix E. So, in this case, SMS is a pretty safe feature to use. You have a much higher risk of forgetting your master password and not being able to recover your account than the risk of a compromised account.

General -> Advanced Settings

Under General hit **"Show Advanced Settings"** and now we get to the good stuff:

Alerts

Passwords Alerts.

Password Alerts   Disable Password Alerts

When Enabled -- which means the button text says, **"Disable Password Alerts"** (yeah, I know, great UI) LastPass will alert you when you use weak or duplicate passwords. I strongly recommend leaving this enabled (the default). It may be annoying when you first use LastPass, but that will encourage you to change all your passwords to be unique and strong.

Re-Prompt for Master Password before doing these actions...

Re-prompt for Master Password

Re-prompt for your LastPass master password:
- ☑ Access an Identity
- ☐ Access a Site's password
- ☐ Access a Site
- ☐ Access a Secure Note
- ☐ Access a Form Fill
- ☐ Log in to a site

It's annoying to have to enter your Master Password over and over so the only box I check above is "Access an identity" which is the default.

Security
Security Email

Security		
Security Email	ben@example.com	Send Test Email

So, this is an interesting and welcome feature. It essentially is a secret email address, different than the one you give out to people. When you have emails sent to you from LastPass that involve multifactor authentication you'll get them at this account.

One reason to enable this is if you think it's likely that someone would compromise your main email account.

Country Restriction

Here you can restrict from which countries you will be able to access your LastPass Account. Select the countries you dwell in or frequently visit. Now that hacker from Bulgaria? Locked out! This isn't foolproof. Professional hackers will relay their attacks through a different country. But security comes in layers like a sandwich and this is an extra layer of protection.

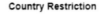 

If you use a <u>Satellite</u> (I pity you) or <u>VPN</u> provider be sure to select those (at the bottom of the **Country Restriction** list). Otherwise leave them unchecked.

Tor Networks

Tor Networks	☑ Prohibit logins from Tor networks

Unless you use Tor, prohibit logins from Tor Networks. Tor is a way to anonymize traffic and is notoriously used by hackers.

Revert Master Password

Revert Master Password	☑ Allow master password changes to be reverted

If you change your Master Password, leaving this checked allows you to revert it to your old password within 30 days. I recommend leaving this checked because you are more likely to forget your Master Password after having just changed it.

Disable Email Verification

Disable Email Verification	☐ Don't require email verification from unknown devices and locations.

Leave this unchecked. It is good to require email verification under these circumstances.

Disable multifactor trust expiration

Disable Multifactor Trust Expiration	☐ Don't end trust period after 30 days.

I would leave this unchecked for better security. If you check it, once a device has been authenticated it doesn't require multi-factor verification every 30 days.

Auto-Logoff Other Devices

Auto-Logoff Other Devices	☐ Log out of other devices upon login from a different device.

I don't see a reason to have this enabled unless you're logging into LastPass on computers you don't own which you should never do.

Password Iterations

Password Iterations	200200

This is the number of times your credentials are hashed. The larger the value the longer it takes to crack your password (and the longer it takes for your computer or phone to open your vault). I suggest a high value but don't go crazy here. LastPass recommends 100100. I always go higher than the recommended like 200200. This may cause problems on older phones.

Website Auto-Logoff and Bookmarklet Auto-Logoff

Website Auto-Logoff	2 Weeks ▼
Bookmarklet Auto-Logoff	2 Weeks ▼

The default value of 2 weeks is fine.

Privacy
Track History

Privacy	
Track History	✔ Keep track of login and form fill history

This is useful to leave enabled so that you can view which sites you've logged into most recently as well as a history of when each login was used.

Help Improve LastPass
This is up to you; I leave it enabled but if you're concerned about error reporting data you can uncheck this.

Tools

Destroy Sessions

This will allow you to logoff any and all LastPass devices on your account.

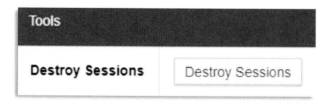

Now, when you press that **"Destroy Sessions"** button...

Actually, you'll just see the next screen with a list of your Active LastPass Sessions:

Delete	Time	User Agent	IP Address	Country
☐	2019-07-26 18:56:56		110.sub-174-216-17.myvzw.com	United States
	2019-07-26 18:48:45		38.146.75.143	United States

Kill checked sessions   **Kill all but current session**

Press the **"Kill checked sessions"** or **"Kill all but current session"** button. Use this to destroy all

LastPass sessions for any and all devices logged into your LastPass account. This is useful if you had a phone or laptop lost or stolen, or if you had to make an emergency trip and wanted to be sure your computer at home was logged out of LastPass. I should note that if your computer or phone is not online it's not going to destroy its LastPass session.

Remove Duplicates

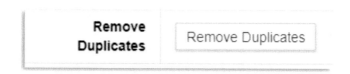

This runs the Duplicate Remover program which will search your Vault for duplicate Items and offers to remove them.

Action Items:

- ✓ **Setup SMS Account Recovery**
- ✓ **Set Country Restrictions**
- ✓ **Disallow logins from Tor Networks**
- ✓ **Increase Password iterations to 200200.**
- ✓ **Run Remove Duplicates**

Multifactor Options

What is Multifactor Authentication?

For the purpose of LastPass, MFA (Multi Factor Authentication) is an additional form of  authentication to identify yourself to LastPass in addition to your password. This is a huge extra layer of security. Remember that security comes in layers like a cake.

If you have multifactor authentication enabled, it is unlikely that a hacker could gain access to your LastPass account EVEN IF he knew your Master Password. Keeping your Master Password confidential is very important. But adding multifactor authentication is your biggest defense against a Master Password compromise.

It is wise to secure your LastPass account with multifactor authentication. In case I wasn't clear in the previous sentence: It is wise to secure your LastPass account with multifactor authentication. You should enable multifactor authentication. I strongly suggest that you enable multifactor authentication. It would be prudent of you to enable multifactor authentication. **Please, enable multifactor authentication!**

Multifactor Option	Name
LastPass•••ı AUTHENTICATOR	LastPass Authenticator
Google Authenticator	Google Authenticator
Microsoft Authenticator	Microsoft Authenticator
toopher	Toopher
DUO	Duo Security
Transakt	Transakt
#	Grid

MFA Options with LastPass

Let's go over some Multifactor Options, there are roughly 3 categories of MFA you can use with LastPass:

1. **App Authenticators**. These are apps on your phone that display a rolling-code which changes every 30 seconds. To login to LastPass you would not only have to enter your normal password, but you would need to open an authenticator app on your phone which would show you the code, then enter it in addition to your password. Examples of apps that do this are: LastPass Authenticator, Google Authenticator, Microsoft Authenticator.

2. **Push Notifications Apps.** These apps allow LastPass to send Push Notifications to your phone with a code. The LastPass Authenticator also features this.

3. **Piece of Paper.** A unique matrix of letters and numbers you can carry around on paper with you to lookup an MFA code. The grid option can do this.

4. **USB Security Keys.** A physical security key that you must insert into your computer's USB port (some of these can also work with a

phone using NFC (Near Field Communication).

What If You Lose the Authenticator?

I know you are asking the obvious question: **If I lose my authenticator; will I lose access to LastPass?** I am glad you asked that question. The answer is "No." If you are already logged into LastPass you can go into Account Settings and disable the authenticator that you lost. Otherwise on the LastPass login screen there is an option to disable the authenticator… in this case LastPass will send you an email to confirm you want to disable it (this will be sent to your Secure Email address if you enabled it, otherwise your normal email). **This essentially means your email always acts as a backup multifactor device.** *Make sure that you keep your email secure.*

Here is a disaster scenario, for your consideration….

Your house catches fire. You get out safely with your family and cats but lose all your computers and phones. You no longer have any MFA devices. How are you going to get into LastPass? **It is good to think through these things** and have a plan for it. Your email can always be used as a multifactor device so my suggestion is to memorize your email password. Not to make things more complicated but most email services like Gmail and Outlook.com also let you protect your email account with multifactor auth… and if those devices have been burned up in the fire how will you login to your email. My suggestion is for any service you enable MFA, especially LastPass and Email, print out some backup codes and store a copy of them at a friend or relative's house.

Tip: Your Email (or your Security Email address if you use it) is the one password you should memorize instead of storing in LastPass because it is the one account you can use to disable MFA on LastPass if you lose all your computers, phones, and MFA devices. Obviously, this email should NOT be protected with MFA. Or better yet, you may enable MFA on your email account if you store printed out backup codes at a different location such as a bank deposit box, or with a trusted friend or relative. It is best to store these codes in a separate geographic location.

What Multifactor Options are Best?

It all depends on your situation, but the three I think are best (and I personally use) are:

1. **LastPass Authenticator** App. The reason I like this is it gives you the option of both rolling codes and push alerts (to which you can just open the app and hit the Approve button) for LastPass login.
2. **Grid**. Grid is a code grid printed on a piece of paper. It's easy to put a few extra copies in safe places in case of a fire.
3. **YubiKey**. I like YubiKey USB hardware tokens. It's simply a $50 USB stick that you can put in your computer and tap it to authenticate with LastPass. You can store it on your keychain with your keys, or a small YubiKey could be left in your computer. YubiKeys are also popular MFA devices for services such as Google and Facebook.

Enabling the LastPass Authenticator

I suggest using the LastPass Authenticator App on your phone. Hit the Edit button under Action:

Set "**Enabled**" to "**Yes**" and decide if you want to "**Permit Offline Access**". For the sake of security, I recommend setting "**Disallow**" for offline access. However, if you will be in situations where you may need to login to your vault while you are offline you should allow it.

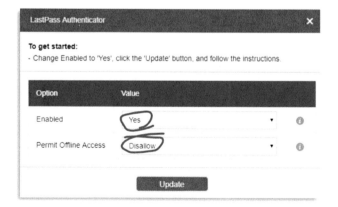

You'll be prompted to **"Enroll"** your phone with LastPass Authenticator.

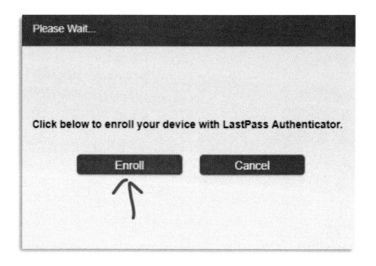

Click **"Set up mobile app"**

And now you can open the LastPass authenticator on your phone and scan the QR code.

Tip: If you have multiple phones that you want to run the Authenticator app on you can scan the QR code into multiple phones.

You'll be prompted to **"Set up text message"** as a backup for MFA.

I would suggest a Google Voice number for the extra security Google Provides.

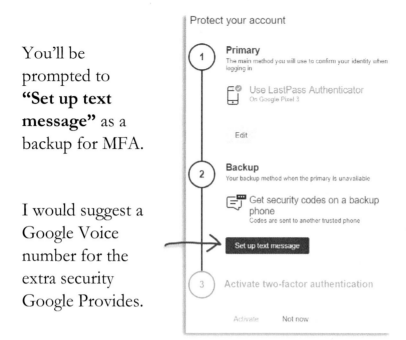

This may be useful if you destroy your phone (losing your QR code). Once you get a new phone you can then receive a text message to recover your account.

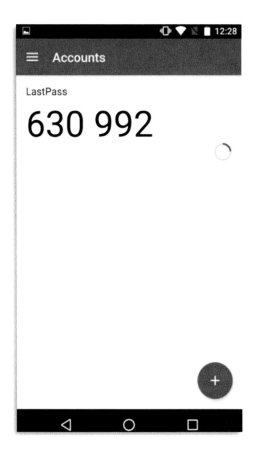

Now the LastPass Authenticator app will display a
rolling code that changes every few seconds. You
will be prompted to enter this code when logging
into LastPass.

Enrolling Grid (Paper MFA in case you destroy your phone)

| # | Grid | Printable spreadsheet of numbers and letters used to enter different values when logging in. | Enabled | |

I strongly suggest enrolling in Grid. That lets you print out a piece of paper which will allow you to login if you lose (or drop) your phone.

The grid paper is a random matrix of codes. When logging into LastPass if you don't have access to your phone you'll be asked for the values of coordinates on the grid. In the example below if LastPass asked you for **E2, L7, and T5** you would enter **j, y, k.**

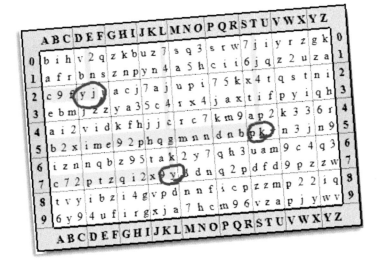

Tip: Print out multiple copies of your Grid. Keep a copy at home and mail one to a trusted relative or friend. It is unlikely that you'll ever need it. But you may need it someday to get into your LastPass account.

Enrolling YubiKey Authentication

Simply select one of the YubiKey fields and touch your YubiKey to fill out the field. Hit the Update button at the bottom to register it with LastPass. You can set up as many as 5 YubiKeys:

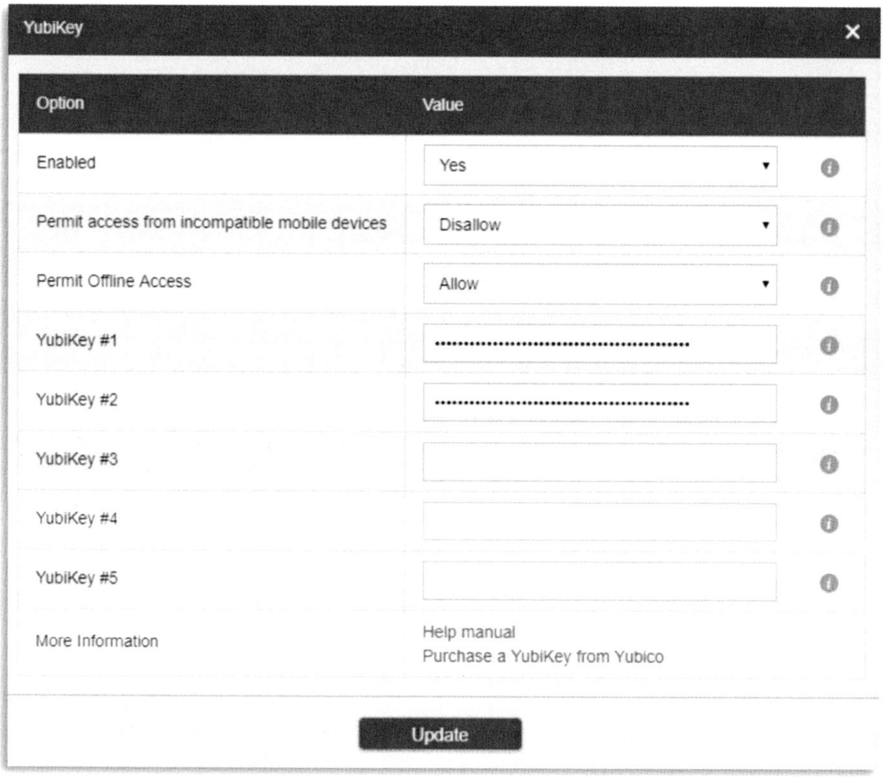

Option	Value	
Enabled	Yes ▾	ⓘ
Permit access from incompatible mobile devices	Disallow ▾	ⓘ
Permit Offline Access	Allow ▾	ⓘ
YubiKey #1	••	ⓘ
YubiKey #2	••	ⓘ
YubiKey #3		ⓘ
YubiKey #4		ⓘ
YubiKey #5		ⓘ
More Information	Help manual Purchase a YubiKey from Yubico	

YubiKey ✕

Update

 Tip: Setting up YubiKeys for use outside of LastPass is beyond the scope of this document, but they can be used as a secure 2nd factor for many services including Google and Facebook and more.

YubiKeys are USB hardware tokens. You can get them in USB-A, USB-C, and even with NFC (Near Field Communication). There are a variety of YubiKeys available here: https://www.yubico.com/store/

These are made in the USA and Sweden and Yubico takes security very seriously—the keys cannot be modified (part of their security design). No security device is perfect—but Yubico stands behind their products. <u>Once there was a potential security issue with one of my YubiKeys and Yubico replaced it free of charge.</u>

I own 2 types of YubiKeys:

My favorite is the **YubiKey 5 NFC.** This device can authenticate with just about anything and even can authenticate wirelessly using NFC by tapping it against Android devices. It can be used for much more than LastPass. It supports FIDO2, U2F, Smart Card (PIV), OTP, OATH HOTP, OATH TOTP, PGP. I haven't found any service it won't work with. I keep this on my keyring.

My second favorite is the **YubiKey 5 Nano.** The only feature it doesn't have is NFC. I always keep this one plugged into my laptop. It is so small it hides away in the USB port almost flush with the computer, and it's just a tap to authenticate to LastPass or websites that support FIDO2.

Action Items:

- ✓ **Enable Multifactor Authentication using the LastPass Authenticator for Android or iPhone.**
- ✓ **Enable Grid, print out several copies and place a copy in a remote location.**

Trusted Devices

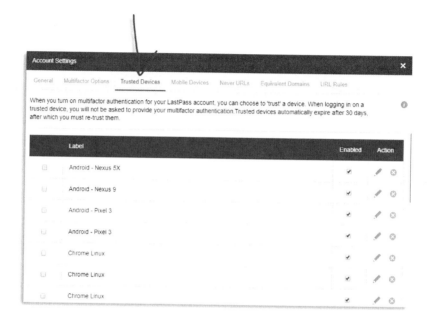

Here is a list of Trusted Devices. I generally trust my devices, so I don't have to provide MFA but every 30 days. There's generally not any reason to change or delete these.

Mobile Devices

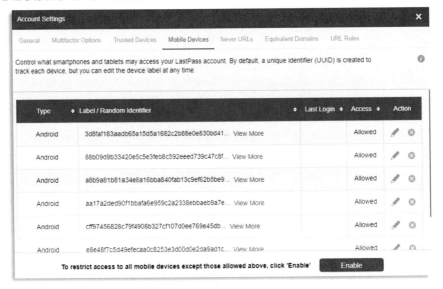

This is a list of Mobile Devices that have accessed your LastPass account. You'll notice at the bottom you could Enable a restriction to all mobile devices except those listed above that you've already logged into. There aren't too many reasons I can think of that you would want to enable that option.

Never URLS

It is extremely rare that LastPass will give you trouble. LastPass is one of the most popular password managers so most of the kinks have been ironed out. That said, if you want to turn off LastPass for a particular website, here's where to do it.

Here you can add sites or URLs where you want LastPass to not do what it normally does. In the example above I added a poorly designed 401k site, it was easier just to copy/paste the credentials from LastPass than to have it autologin. Out of the billions of sites I have in LastPass, I believe that's the only site it has ever had trouble with.

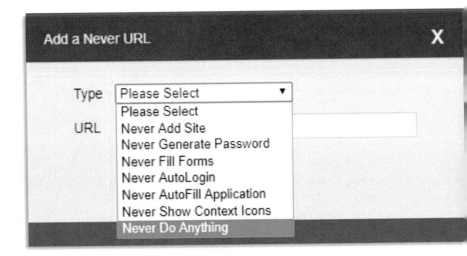

When you add a Never URL you have the **following options**:

- ✓ **Never Add a Site** – LastPass will not create a new password entry when visiting this URL.
- ✓ **Never Generate Password** – LastPass won't auto-generate a password when changing a password on this URL.

- ✓ **Never Fill Forms** – LastPass will not enable Form Fills on this URL.
- ✓ **Never AutoLogin** – Will still fill in your password fields but won't login for you.
- ✓ **Never AutoFill Application** – I'm not sure when you would use this since an application isn't a URL.
- ✓ **Never Show Context Icons** – Don't show the LastPass icons over the login fields on this site.
- ✓ **Never Do Anything** – Essentially disables LastPass for this URL.

In the URL field you can use the keyword "all" to disable a feature on every site.

Equivalent Domains

LastPass has the ability to recognize when multiple websites use the same credentials. Google.com and YouTube.com is a good example of this. LastPass has most of them predefined as Global entries, but here you can add more.

You'll notice I added 3 custom equivalent domain entries:

1. Logos.com and Biblia.com share the same login info.
2. All the Stack Exchange sites share the same login info.

3. OpenDNS.com and DNSOmatic.com share the same login info.

Without equivalent domains, multiple websites that share the same credentials would create multiple entries in LastPass and then when you changed your password the other entries wouldn't get the update. What a pain that would be!

URL Rules

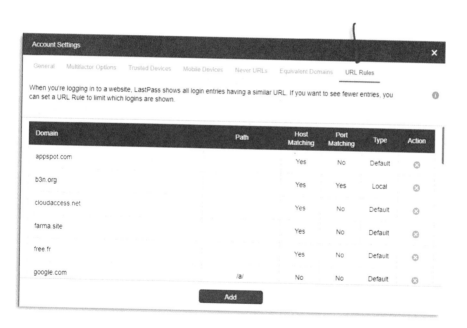

You will probably not need to do anything with URL Rules. But here you can be very granular about exactly how a URL is matched to present a login. Above I added my b3n.org domain

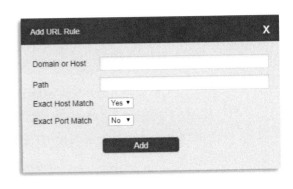

with port matching because I sometimes run services on alternative ports on my LAN that have separate logins.

Chapter 10: Manage Family

If you are using LastPass for Families, you'll see a "Managing Family" option on the left menu. Here you can hit the **Add Family Member** button and add up to 5 total family members (6 including yourself).

Each member of your family has their own personal password vault. You will not be able to see each other's personal password vaults. But you can create a Shared Folder visible to some or all of your family members and your family members will be able to see passwords stored in the folder for which they have access.

Add Member   ✕

Email address

eli@example.com

First name

Eli

Last name

Bryan

Press the Add Family Member Button, then fill in your family member's email, first, and last names.

Your family member will receive an email like below.

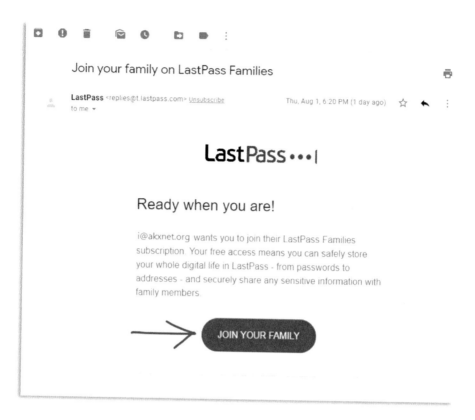

Have them hit the "Join Your Family" button to accept the invitation and they'll be prompted to login to their LastPass account (or create one if they don't have one). Each of your family members will have their own LastPass Account associated with their own email address.

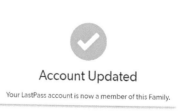

Account Updated

Your LastPass account is now a member of this Family.

Once they've accepted, back at the manage family screen, **click on their name to set their role**. Two roles are available: **Member** or **Family Manager**. The latter can add and remove family members. I suggest making the parents Family Managers and the rest Members.

Please note that Family Managers do not have access to other family member's personal vaults. In order to share credentials, they must be placed in a Shared Folder or the Password Items must be shared individually.

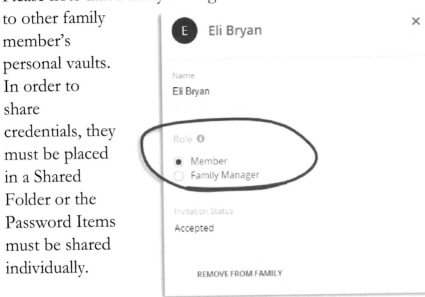

Action Item:

   ✓ **Add a family member**

Chapter 11: Sharing Center

Vault → Left Side
Menu → Sharing
Center

This brings us to the
Sharing Center.

The Sharing Center is a way to securely share
passwords with your family, or with others outside
the family (if you're using one of the Business Plans
you can replace the word family with coworkers).
Even though the passwords are shared, they are
encrypted in such a way that only people who have
access to the shared folders or items can decrypt
them. This works using public/private key
cryptography. I won't get into the details here, but I
just want to note that because of the way this is
designed, LastPass employees will not be able to
access your passwords even though they are shared.
Only those with whom the password is shared can
decrypt the data.

Manage Shared Folders

When you open the Sharing Center the first thing you'll notice is the Manage Shared Folders section.

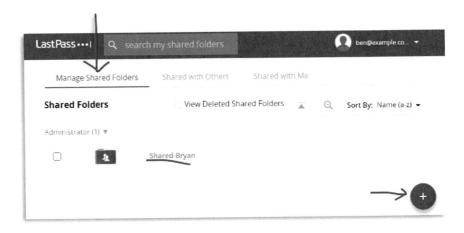

Here you can see I already have a folder called Shared-Bryan. This is where I share data for the Bryan Family. Of course, I can add as many Shared Folders as I want. Let's hit the red + sign on the bottom right to add a new Shared Folder…

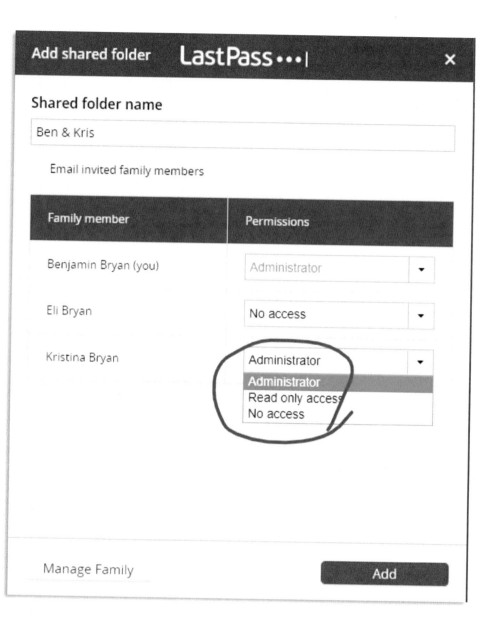

You can see above I created a Shared Folder that only Kris & I have access to but Eli does not. The

Folder access you can give each family member are:

- ✓ **Administrator** – can add, edit, delete, and view password items.
- ✓ **Read only access** - can view passwords but not modify or delete them
- ✓ **No access** – no access to this password folder.

I suggest giving most family members **Administrator** access to folders, that way if they need to change the password or add notes to the password entry it's easy for them to do so.

Once you have created a **Shared Folder** you and your family will be able to see it in LastPass under the **Sharing Center**. But if you look in your vault you won't see the folder! That's because you haven't added any password items to it yet. Open your Vault (go to All Items) and expand a password entry you want to share with your Family…

Then hover over the password entry and hit the wrench to edit:

Change the folder to your Shared Folder and hit Save.

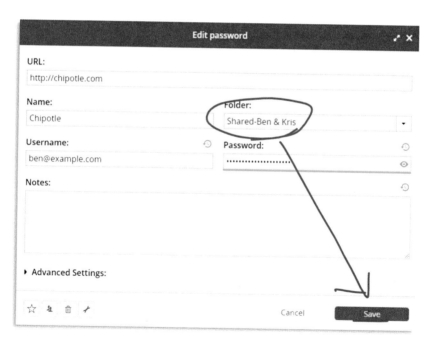

LastPass warns you that other people will now be able to view the password, to share you will want to click **"Yes"**.

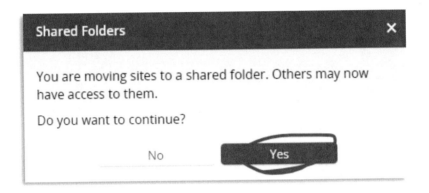

Now in your Vault You'll see the Shared Password folder. LastPass convention is to always prefix a shared folder with "Shared-" so it's very obvious which folders you are sharing.

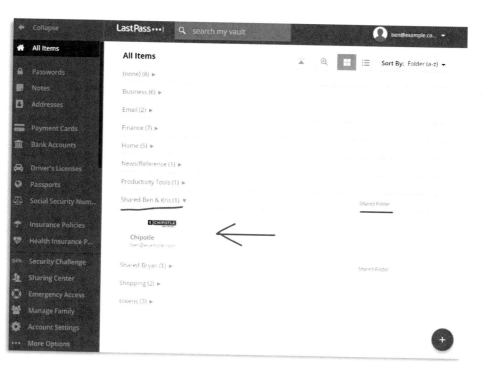

You can also Drag and Drop other Password Items
into a Shared Folder to share with other members of
the family.

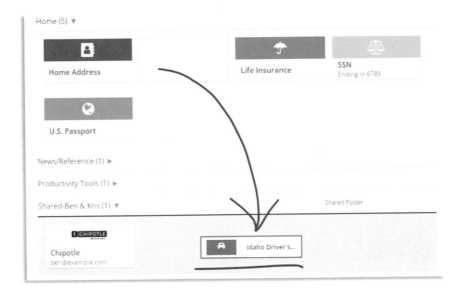

LastPass Guide

Shared with Others

This is a little different than folders. This allows you to share individual items that are not in a Shared Folder. An example to this is I may send an Excel Document encrypted with a password to a customer, and I want to share just that one password with them. Items can be shared with anyone, even people outside of your Family or Work.

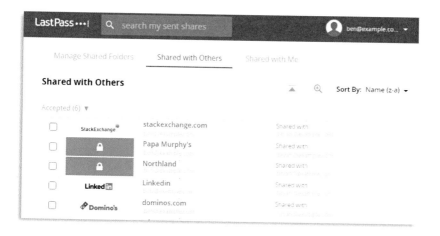

Hitting the plus on the bottom-right you can share items that are in your vault.

Enter a recipient email address, you typically want to allow the Recipient to view the password (If you leave this unchecked, they can access a website by launching it from LastPass but can't view the password easily.)

On the right under Items to Share hit the dropdown and select or type (autocomplete works here) a name of a password item. You can select multiple items. In the example below I am going to share two password Items: **Azure Frontend Server** and **Azure SQL DB1**. Hit Share. Your recipient will have an opportunity to Accept the Share Offer and then he'll see the password in his vault.

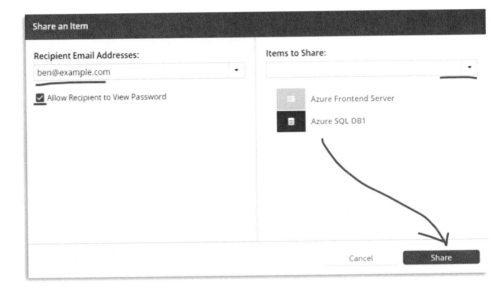

Another way to Share is by hitting the Sharing Icon on a Password Entry:

When you first share something with someone it is in a Pending status until they accept the Share Offer. The recipient will receive an email and can click the **"Accept"** button there, or in LastPass hover over the pending entry and an **"Accept"** Button will show up.

If the recipient does not see the incoming Share Offer right way, have him force a refresh. Hit the LastPass extension icon in the browser, Account Options → Advanced → Refresh sites.

Shared with Me

The last tab is the same as the above, but the other way around. This shows you passwords that have been shared with you.

If someone shares a new item with you, you'll receive a notification on the left bar on the Sharing Center. Click on that....

Then Accept the Share. Once you do, you'll see it in your Vault.

Action Items:

- ✓ **Create a Shared Folder and Share it with a Family Member**
- ✓ **Share an Individual Password Item with someone**

Chapter 12: Emergency Access

Left pane → Emergency Access

 And just as it is appointed for man to die once, and after that comes judgment. – Hebrews 9:27 ESV

One thing that we can be confident in is our mortality. We do not know when our appointed time will come, it could be later today or 100 years from now. But come it will. Along with having a will and trust, we should also have a plan for our passwords; this will make things so much easier on your family if they can just get access to your LastPass account.

This is one of the most valuable Premium / Family plan features about LastPass. Emergency Access ($) allows you to designate a trusted person to gain access to your LastPass account after you die. And not only death, but incapacitation, or even the scenario where you forgot your master password and lost access to your email and have no way to reset it.)

People I Trust

In LastPass you can add a person you trust. **A person you trust can gain access to all the passwords if something unexpected happens to you.** In general, it's a good idea to add your husband or wife. But one can add a trusted friend (even if they do not have a LastPass Premium account). If you are using LastPass for business use only you may want to add your business partner.

What this does is every password in your vault is encrypted so that the master password of the person(s) you trust can decrypt it—but even though they have the ability to decrypt your passwords, they don't have access to your passwords. LastPass won't give them access to your passwords until they request access. After a person you trust requests access, they must **wait** for the waiting period to expire. During the wait period LastPass will send you multiple email alerts. You may decline their request. If you don't decline it, after the waiting period expires, they will automatically gain full access to your account.

 Tip on choosing a waiting Period for your Emergency Access Trusted Person: Should you pick immediately? One day, 30 days, or something in between? I think it's best to pick a timeframe less than immediate. You don't want to pick a time period so short you don't have a chance to stop it; or so long it doesn't give your trusted contact access soon enough. Pick a timeframe that gives you enough time to stop an Emergency Access request. If you frequently go on 1-week sabbaticals from your computer, choose a time period longer than 1 week.

Here's an example:

Your husband Josh is a person you trust. You end up in the hospital, in a coma for several months. In the meantime, Josh needs to pay the water bill, a task you usually did ... but you never thought to share the water company password with him. Josh can request Emergency Access to your LastPass account. If you had setup a 2-day waiting period, he must wait 2 days then LastPass will grant him access to your vault. Now Josh won't die of dehydration while you recover.

I must take my hat off to LastPass! The Emergency Access feature is a job well done.

The Passwords are encrypted in such a way that only the people you trust can decrypt them, but they can't access them. LastPass has no way to decrypt them but can grant access. And LastPass won't allow the people you trust to access your passwords when they request access until the waiting period expires giving you a chance to stop it.

With Emergency Access your passwords are available to loved ones when needed but are still **protected by the two-man rule**: The person you trust and LastPass must both agree to give the person you trust access to the passwords.

People Who Trust Me

The **People Who Trust Me** tab shows people who trust you with Emergency Access to their account.

If something unexpected should happen to them where you need to gain access to their passwords, simply hover over their email which will cause a **"Request Access"** button to appear.

Demonstration

Eli has setup Ben as a person that he trusts with a 3-hour waiting period.

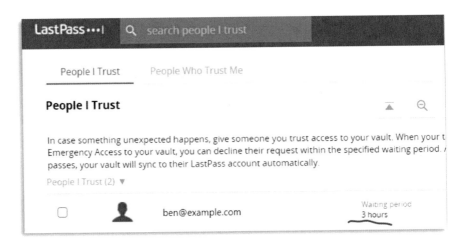

Eli travels overseas, and his Passport and phone get stolen. He needs a copy of his Passport emailed to the Consulate but can't login to LastPass without his phone. Fortunately, Eli scanned a copy of his Passport into LastPass. He contacts Ben who requests Emergency Access to Eli's Account.

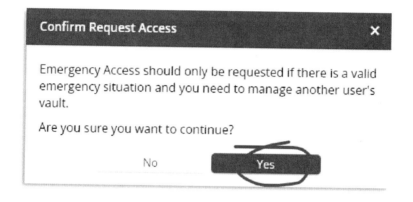

Access pending until
8/3/2019, 1:25:00 PM

What happens next?

Eli will receive an email from LastPass

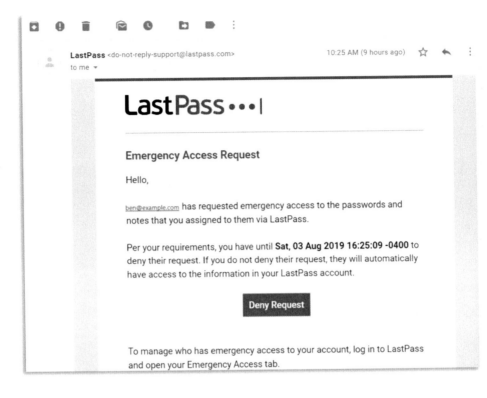

During the waiting period LastPass will send multiple emails to Eli each day. He can't miss it if he's checking email and wants to stop it.

Once the waiting period is over, Ben will be able to see Eli's passwords in his Vault:

LastPass Guide

Ben can open Eli's passport and send a copy to the consulate.

Ben can also see that his account is linked to Eli's on the **People Who Trust Me** tab. When access is no longer needed Ben can move the mouse over the entry and an option to unlink it pops up. Likewise, Eli will see his account is linked on *his* **People I Trust** tab and he can unlink it from there.

Note that once the account is unlinked Ben will no longer be able to request Emergency Access, Eli will need to re-add Ben as an Emergency Access contact.

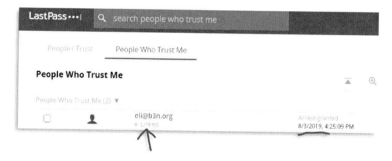

Action Item:

✓ **Setup a Person that you Trust in the Emergency Access Section.**

Chapter 13: Security Dashboard

Left Pane → Security Dashboard

LastPass includes a Security Dashboard which will help you make your accounts more secure.

The **Security Dashboard** feature of LastPass scans all your password entries and challenges you to improve them. It also checks them for issues. Here are some of the main things it will look for:

- **Compromised Passwords** – LastPass checks for websites and services you use that may have been compromised (hacked, or leaked credentials, etc.).
- **Weak Passwords** – Passwords that are too short or easy to guess
- **Reused Passwords** – It is best practice to not use the same password on multiple websites. If you have, it will show up here. See also the chapter on Equivalent Domains.
- **Old Passwords** – Good security practice is to change your passwords regularly. This is a list of passwords LastPass deems too old.

Okay, **I am going to let you in on a secret.** I haven't looked at my Security Score since LastPass introduced the feature. I don't know how bad it looks. But I'm not going to clean it up for the sake of writing this guide because I want you to see how messy it is for someone like me that takes security seriously—I want you to see that I'm not perfect…

Here it is (turn the page)…

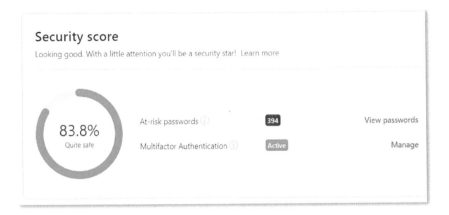

This is my actual report (whew, not as bad as I thought). You can see I'm doing pretty good with a Security Score of 83.8%! It's not perfect, but there are always tradeoffs and I've chosen to be less secure in some situations.

View Passwords

Click on "View Passwords" on the At-risk passwords row and it will take you to the screen below…

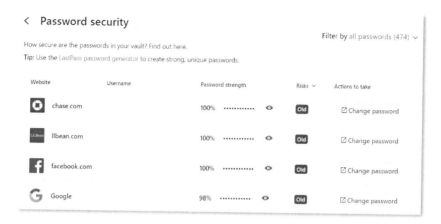

This shows some opportunities where I could improve my score.

In full transparency, I have some Weak and Reused passwords that I can't fix. This is embarrassing, but it's the reality. Most of my weak and reused passwords are on my internal facing LAN so it's not best practice but also not the end of the world. There are always security vs. convenience tradeoffs and sometimes I choose convenience when it is appropriate to do so.

But I do have some old passwords I should take care of now. I can hit the "Change password" button to take me right to the site needed to reset my old or weak passwords.

Lastly, at the very bottom of the report is a Dark web Monitoring section. If your email address says, "Not Monitored" hover your mouse over it and click "Start Monitoring." LastPass will monitor your email address for any compromises or security breaches. You'll receive an alert like the below if one of your accounts using that email address has public a security incident:

Dark web monitoring

1 email address appeared in a known security breach.

ben@b3n.org `Compromised`

This will let you know if an online account using your email address is ever found with a compromised password. Usually this happens if one of your online services gets compromised.

You will also get an email, the email will show you a list of incidents where you have had information compromised. Either your data was leaked, your email address exposed, your password hashes uploaded, etc.

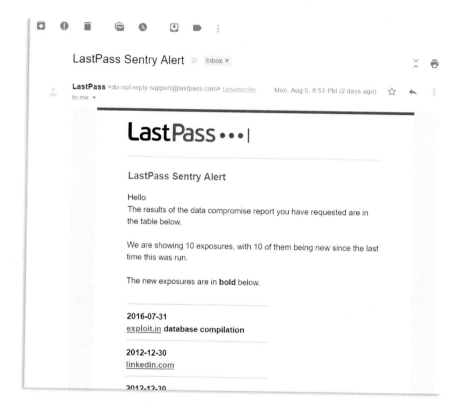

Usually the best course of action is to make sure you've changed the password on websites with known vulnerabilities if you haven't done so since the vulnerability was discovered. Consider that password compromised and change it. If you were using that same password on multiple sites (like you should not have been) make sure to change it on any site that used that password.

Action Item:

- ✓ **View your Security Dashboard**
- ✓ **Change Weak Passwords.**

Chapter 14: More Options

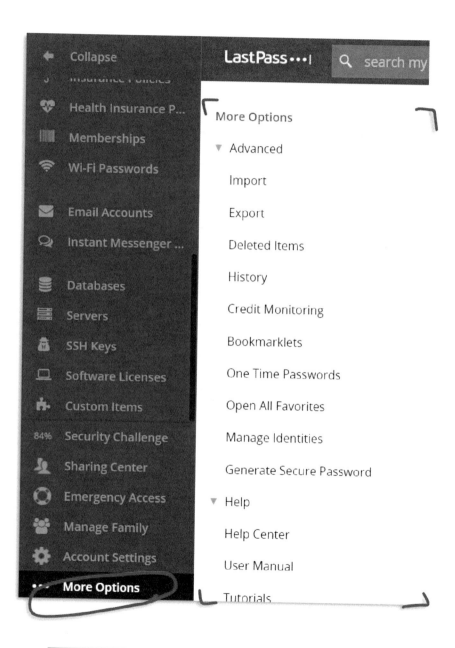

I'll briefly go over more options. Most of these you won't ever need but may be of interest in case you need them.

Import
Import Passwords from another Password Manager.

Export
Export Passwords to a File

Deleted Items
A list of items you have deleted from the vault. Here you can restore entries by hovering over an item and hitting the restore button.

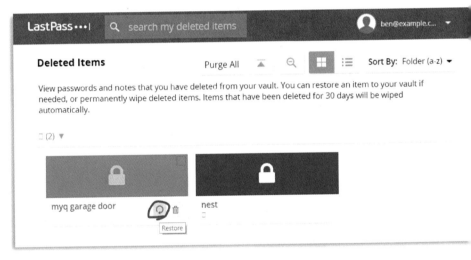

Items that are in the Deleted Items folder will be purged after 30 days.

Credit Monitoring

Left Pane → More Options → Advanced → Credit Monitoring

Here is something of interest. LastPass Premium and Family subscribers can get Free Credit Monitoring with LastPass.

But usefulness here is limited… you can see from the screenshot I got an alert on 2019-04-10 about a "Critical Change". So, the free service isn't very useful because I have to upgrade to LastPass's $9.95/month credit monitoring service to see what the Critical Change actually is!

If you do want to enable this free Credit Monitoring service hit the red plus (+) button → Create New Profile. Then create a new Credit Monitoring Profile:

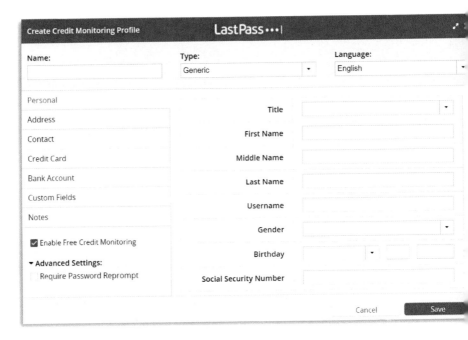

While it's nice to have Free Credit Monitoring with LastPass, I don't see a good reason to use it. For free services https://www.creditkarma.com offers much more than LastPass's free Credit Monitoring.

One Time Passwords (OTP)

A One Time Password provides a way for you to login to your LastPass account with a password that you can only use once. The reason you may want to do this is if you had to login to LastPass in a situation where other people may intercept your password. A typical scenario is if you think you may be under video surveillance and someone could record your keystrokes, or in an area where you suspect a Tempest Attack—someone monitoring for electromagnetic emissions for example could read your keystrokes remotely and intercept your Master Password. You could use a One Time Password in this scenario to avoid revealing your Master Password. However, **if you suspect these sorts of attacks it may be better to just not login to LastPass (or even turn on your computer) until you're in a safer area.** That said, here is how to use a one-time password:

Go to this page: https://lastpass.com/otp.php click the "Add a new One time Password" button.

ONE TIME PASSWORDS

One Time Passwords

Help

To login using a One Time Password, you must always use this page. You can reach this page from the Sign in link on the homepage, then One Time Passwords button.

Add a new One Time Password   Clear all OTPs   Print

You have no One Time Passwords, you can make some above

You'll get a One Time Password (below). If you want more than one, hit the button several times until you have enough. Then you can print them out.

1.   65dbab67453b7660c2f6ea2a925abbeb

Next time you want to login using a One Time Password access this site: https://lastpass.com/otp.php and enter in one of the passwords. Once you use it, cross it off the list. <u>It will never work again.</u>

 Don't Do This: I have heard of people using the One Time Password feature to login to LastPass on computers they don't trust such as a cybercafé, hotel or library computer. I strongly discourage doing this. If a computer is possibly compromised, malicious software can dump the contents of memory—and if you're logged into LastPass it could dump the passwords of all your accounts. Please only use LastPass with your own personal computer. If your computer gets damaged or stolen, don't even think about logging into LastPass on a public computer. Buy a new computer before you access LastPass again.

Open All Favorites

This option opens all websites that you have marked as a favorite. A rather useless feature.

Manage Identities

Here is a useful feature. LastPass allows you to setup multiple Identities under an account. The way I use this is I setup a "Home" identity for my personal accounts, and I setup separate identity for each client or organization with whom I do contract or volunteer work. To create an Identity hit the plus (+) button.

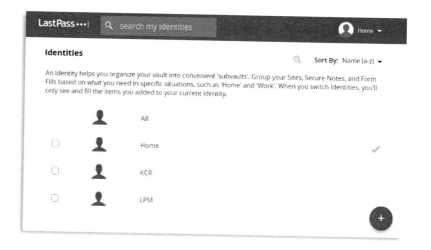

Tip: Before using LastPass to store account information for a client or employer, check with the IT Department or Information Security Department to make sure LastPass is an approved solution.

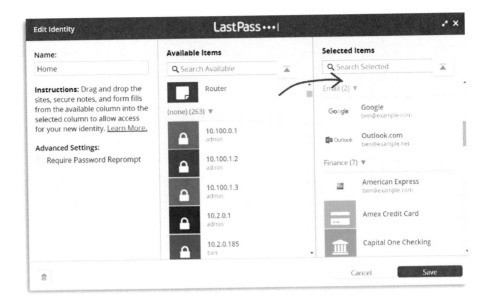

Here you can select which items are selected for that identity. Just drag and drop items from Available to Selected.

One reason it's wise to setup multiple identities is if I walk away from my computer and forget to lock my screen an opportunistic hacker would be limited to whatever Identity I have open.

 Now, you should never leave your computer unlocked, and never leave it unattended. But like I have said before, security comes in layers like bricks.

If someone down the hall yells "Help!" you're going to rush to their aid and may forget to lock your computer first (locking your computer when you walk away is your first layer of defense so always lock your computer). If you have LastPass open that may be just enough time for a hacker to quickly get your banking credentials while you're not looking. But with Identities there's one more layer for someone to get through to get to all your accounts.

How you use Identities is best determined by you. One simple suggestion is to have an Identity for all your financial accounts and another identity for less important accounts.

 Tip: It is good security practice to get into the habit of locking your computer whenever you walk away. In Windows hit the Windows+L keys simultaneously and your computer will instantly lock. On Mac this is Command+Control+Q. I habitually lock my screen whenever I walk away.

Even if it weren't for the security aspect, just the organization is worth using Identities.

Your current Identity is shown in the top-right of LastPass.

To Switch Identities click the Identity in the top right, then you can select from your identities. If you select "All" You will be able to see the passwords in all identities.

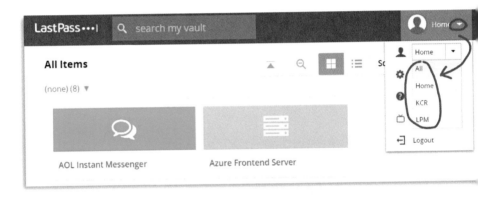

Chapter 15: Don't Leave LastPass Open Unattended!

Please read my security best practices (Appendix E). But the number one security mistake I see people make is not securing LastPass when they walk away.

You leave your computer unlocked with guests over, or your computer gets stolen and LastPass is still logged into the browser… that's bad.

Two quick ways to protect yourself (either one will work, I only use the first option, but you can use both for extra security).

1. Make sure your computer is set to require a password every time you wake it up (this is found in System Settings → Sign in Options).

2. LastPass icon → Account Options → Extension Preferences →General → Security → Enable log out when all browsers are closed and Log out after this many minutes of inactivity.

General

Notifications

HotKeys

Advanced

Icons

Security

☑ Log out when all browsers are closed

☑ Log out after this many minutes of inactivity 15

General

Appendix A: Threats and Protections Against Them

LastPass is not a foolproof password management system. There are none that are hacker-proof. But it is a reasonably secure password manager that balances security with convenience.
Here are some threats I identified for myself (yours may be different but this should give you some ideas). I ranked each threat against four options: LastPass, KeePass (an offline Password manager), a paper Notebook, and keeping passwords in my head. For my situation LastPass was the best option.

This is a very crude unscientific rating system:

Green = Threat is mitigated, Yellow = Partial mitigation, Red = No mitigation

Threats	LastPass	KeePass	Notebook	Your Head
Forgetting your Master Password	✓	✗	✓	✓
Attack on Master Password	✗	◐	✓	✓
Security Bugs	✗	◐	✓	✓
Natural Disasters	✓	✗	✗	✓
Physical Theft	✓	✗	✗	✗
Family Access in case of Death	✓	✗	◐	✗
Government	✗	◐	◐	◐
Using the Same Credentials Everywhere	✓	✓	◐	✗
Forgetting your Passwords	✓	✓	✓	✗
Not Choosing Strong Passwords	✓	✓	◐	✗
Notifications about compromised sites	✓	✗	✗	✗
Sharing passwords insecurely	✓	✗	✗	✗
OS Compromise	✗	✗	◐	◐
Browser Compromise	✗	◐	◐	◐
Internet is down and need your PIN	◐	✓	✓	✓
Hard Drive Crashes	✓	✗	✓	✓
You lose your notebook/device	✓	✗	✗	✓
House catches fire	✓	✗	✗	✓
Lost time resetting passwords	✓	✓	✓	✗
Lost time sharing passwords	✓	✗	✗	✗

Forgetting Your Master Password

This can be a serious problem for LastPass users. But it can be mitigated with some of the ways LastPass allows for resetting your Master Password.

Attack on Master Password

A weak password is a serious threat. The best protection against this is to pick a very strong Master Password. The threat is somewhat mitigated by multi-factor authentication.

Security Bugs

In the past some security bugs have been found in LastPass that could lead to a password compromise. These sorts of bugs have been patched quickly but the threat remains, and I would say this is LastPass's largest threat.

Natural Disasters

The fact that LastPass stores your data in the cloud means you should be protected from losing passwords in Natural Disasters.

Physical Theft

Because LastPass is stored in the cloud you will not lose your passwords to physical theft.

Family Access in case of Death

LastPass Provides Emergency Access. One of the best features of LastPass.

Governmental

Recently, the DEA (Drug Enforcement Agency) made a demand of LastPass to hand over logins for a LastPass user who was suspected of dealing drugs. LastPass was unable to hand the passwords over (because they were encrypted) but was able to hand over other data such as IP addresses and account information.[**]

If you are concerned about Nation States gaining access to your passwords, you should not use LastPass. While LastPass encrypts your passwords, your information is not entirely safe from the government:

[**] https://www.forbes.com/sites/thomasbrewster/2019/04/10/what-happened-when-the-dea-demanded-passwords-from-lastpass

1. If the government requested LastPass to provide your LastPass data, while it would be encrypted LastPass can still provide metadata on your account. E.g. your IP address history, a list of sites you access, your history, your email address, etc.
2. A Nation State would more likely compromise your computer directly and install a fake version of LastPass that they control.
3. A Nation State would have unlimited resources to get access to your LastPass account. They could get your encrypted data from LastPass, then bribe or threaten one of your trusted contacts to get their master password which of course would be able to decrypt your account.

In short, if your threat is the Government, especially a powerful nation such as the United States or Russia, etc. you should not use LastPass. I should also note that in most cases the government will not need LastPass to gain access to your accounts; they can do this via other means. What I mean by this is if they want to freeze your bank account funds, they'll just call the bank.

Using the Same Credentials Everywhere

LastPass makes it very easy to avoid doing this by randomly generating passwords and warning you when duplicates are found.

Forgetting your Passwords
This is the entire point of LastPass

Not Choosing Strong Passwords
The LastPass Random password generator helps with this, LastPass can also warn you when you have weak passwords.

Notifications about compromised sites
LastPass will notify you if a site you login to has been compromised and you need to reset your password.

Sharing Passwords Insecurely
LastPass provides a way to do this securely but only with other LastPass users.

OS Compromise
An OS compromise means anything on your computer can be compromised. LastPass cannot protect against this.

Browser Compromise
LastPass cannot protect against this. If your browser is compromised so is LastPass.

Internet is down and you need a password entry
LastPass has an offline mode, but it is more likely you'll be in this situation with LastPass than other

methods. Make sure to allow and test offline access if you will need it.

Hard Drive Crashes

LastPass stores your data in the cloud so not an issue. (If this happens, destroy your drive, do not throw it away.)

You Lose Your Notebook / Device

LastPass data is in the cloud. It is important to note that as long as you practice good security (such as locking your devices when not in use, encrypting the drive, and remote wiping a lost or stolen device) you should be safe from all but the most determined hackers from attempting to access your LastPass data. To be ultra-safe it would be best to reset your master password and all your passwords if you have a device stolen.

House Catches Fire

Having the data stored in the cloud will protect you here

Lost Time Resetting Passwords

I consider this a threat to time; over the course of my life how many days will be spent resetting passwords?

Lost Time Sharing Passwords

Same thing; how many days will be spent trying to communicate passwords securely over the phone?

Appendix B: Ways to Use LastPass

AutoFill

I store all my credit cards and mailing addresses in LastPass. When I need to fill one out on a website right-click and fill.

Identities

I use identity management when working on different client projects which makes it easy to only see the credentials I need.

Moving?

I can't tell you how many times it has come in handy to have a list of every bank, company, organization, and government entity I need to update with my physical address just by going through my list of LastPass items.

Insurance Policies

Having insurance information and policy numbers readily available is invaluable. Health, Home, Auto, Life, Disability. It's all at my fingertips. Sometimes when you're in the middle of buying a house or moving you just need that information and it doesn't do you any good if your papers are packed up in boxes.

Software License Keys

Every time I purchase software that requires a license or serial key it goes into LastPass.

Wi-Fi Passwords

Computers and phones are great at remembering Wi-Fi Passwords… until you get a new device. I store Wi-Fi passwords in LastPass. This way the next time I'm at that location with a new computer or phone I don't have to go asking around for the Wireless Password again.

Door Codes, Combination Locks, Pins, Codes, etc.

Whether it's a door code, PIN, a combination lock, or EIN number, I store these in LastPass for ready access.

Appendix C: Trans-Border Traveling

It is not unheard of for border control agencies to compel travelers to unlock a password app such as LastPass. Travelers are sometimes asked to divulge credentials. This could potentially result in a compromise of any of your accounts including your banking accounts.

Some Password Managers have a travel mode which disables the majority of your credentials while traveling. LastPass does not have this feature. I suggest deleting the LastPass app before transiting any border. You can reinstall the app once on the other side.

 Tip: If at any point in time while crossing a border you lose physical control of your computer or phone, that device can no longer be trusted. Throw it away and buy a new one.

Appendix D: LastPass Alternatives

KeePass

KeePass is a free and open source program. It is very good. It is local only, however you can store the KeePass files on a cloud drive such as Google Drive or OneDrive. I used to use KeePass. My main reason for moving away from it is a lack of sharing capabilities, and a lack of the Emergency Access feature, and the browser integration is not as good. However if you don't want or need those features it is a very good option. Arguably since KeePass doesn't store passwords in the cloud it is more secure from online hackers, but also has a greater risk of data loss if proper backups are not maintained.

Bitwarden

Bitwarden is an open source password manager with a free and paid tier. It is lacking some of the more advanced features of LastPass such as Emergency Access. You can host it yourself if you don't trust their servers. I see the largest disadvantages being that (1) it is not as widely used or audited for security vulnerabilities as LastPass and (2) doesn't have the same resources to audit, monitor, and thwart hacking attempts. That said, Bitwarden is an excellent alternative.

1Password

1Password is the most comparable option to LastPass. It lacks the Emergency Access feature and it is slightly more expensive. The largest advantage 1Password has is a Travel Mode. See Appendix C: Trans-Border Traveling.

Appendix E: Essential Security Layers

Security comes in layers like the earth. Here are the most essential layers. Each one by itself may not stop an attacker, but with enough layers if a hacker penetrates one layer she'll just be stopped at the next. **The more layers you take seriously the more effort and resources it will take for a hacker to compromise your data.** We all make mistakes and let our guard down from time to time. But the more security layers you have in place the more likely your data will remain safe.

Strong LastPass Master Password

Having a master password that is long, unique, and not easily guessable is the most important layer of defense.

Automatic Backups

Backups are a must. Backups should be located offsite to protect your data in case of a local disaster (such as a fire or earthquake) and should also be versioned in case your files become infected. One easy way to setup backups is if you have an

Office365 subscription you have 1TB of storage and can automatically backup your documents to OneDrive. No amount of security is foolproof, so if at some time down the road you get ransomware or malware that infects all your files, having the ability to rollback your files to a previous date is invaluable. Having backups may save you from having to pay a hacker thousands of dollars for your files or losing all your data.

Security Updates

Keep your **computer** and **phone** and **browser** up to date. Whether it is Windows, Mac OSX, Linux, Android, or iPhone you simply cannot use out of date software. Nowa-days Windows 10 keeps itself updated automatically. If you are using Windows 7 or older you should upgrade now. Phones are a bit trickier. Most will provide updates once a month or once a quarter. Unfortunately, I have never seen a phone tell you when it is considered end-of-life for security updates. I would suggest that if you have not seen an update for your phone in 90 days it is not getting updates and it is time to replace it. Apple iPhones are known to provide security updates for a long time. For Android phones security longevity is a hit or miss depending on the manufacturer, carrier, and phone model. Most will support their phone for only 2-3 years so you should plan on replacing your phone that often. For Android I would suggest only buying phones on Android's Enterprise Recommended phones: https://www.android.com/enterprise/recommended/ and try to buy a phone that has been released within the last 6-12 months and is running the latest version of Android.

Use a Unique Random Password for every site

LastPass will help you with this. You should never use the same password on multiple sites. The reason is if a hacker compromises one you can almost guarantee he's going to try that login credential on every popular site, especially banking sites. Also your passwords should be randomly generated.

Use a Secure Browser

Chrome, Edge, Firefox, Opera, Brave, or Safari are all secure options and receive frequent security fixes. Fortunately, most browsers keep themselves up to date automatically.

Limit USB Port Usage

A computer can be compromised within seconds at the hardware layer via USB. Limit the USB devices you use. Make sure you're buying from trusted sources. Don't buy used keyboards and mice. Don't let people share files with you via USB. We've got email, DropBox, OneDrive, Google Drive; There's no reason to physically share files. Don't do it. Consider buying some Lindy USB Port Blockers: https://www.amazon.com/Lindy-USB-Port-Blocker-40452/dp/B000I2JWJA to slow down anyone trying to gain USB access to your computer.

Secure Wireless Peripherals

If you use a wireless mouse or keyboard (especially a keyboard) make sure the data between the keyboard and computer is secure. Apple, Microsoft, and Logitech are known to provide security updates for their keyboards and mice when vulnerabilities are found.

Always maintain Physical Possession of Your Devices

Do not lose physical control of your devices. If you lose sight of your phone or computer, you do not know if someone has inserted a USB device into it and compromised it. Re-installing the OS will not make it safe, since USB can infect at the hardware level. A device in this situation cannot be trusted anymore. You'll just have to throw it away and buy a new one. Never let anyone borrow your phone or computer. I never even let guests onto my computer.

Don't Share Your Computer – Have a Guest Computer

I have a dedicated guest computer in my house to let visitors use if they need one. That way they can still print off boarding passes, check their email, or whatever they need to do without risk to my computer.

Limit the number of Apps you install on your phone

The more apps you install the greater your surface area of exposure to potential malware which could hijack your passwords. Stick to well-known popular apps. I suggest not installing any app with less than a million installs and only use the Google Play Store (for Android) or Apple store (for iOS). If you must install a lot of apps or games then it's best to have a dedicated phone for such insecure activity (tied to a different Google or Apple account).

Require a password to unlock your computer

Your computer should always remain locked and password protected when not in use. **Windows+L** or **Command+Control+Q** will instantly lock your screen.

Require a password to unlock your phone

Android and iOS can be set to require a password when unlocking the screen, and the phone should be set to automatically lock after x number of minutes. There are a couple things I should mention here:

- Android has a feature called Smart Lock which allows the phone to remain unlocked in certain conditions. Here are some of the options available on Android:
  - On Body Detection. Once your phone is unlocked it will remain unlocked while it's on your body. Once you put it down it will require a password to unlock.
  - Trusted Places. Keeps your phone unlocked when you are inside a specific area (such as your Home or Office).
  - Trusted Devices. Keeps your phone unlocked as long as you are in proximity with a specific device. It could be your car's Bluetooth for example).
  - Trusted Face. Unlock your device with your face.
  - Trusted Voice. Unlock your device with your voice.

    None of these Smart Lock options are as secure as password but are more convenient. A dedicated hacker could find a picture of your face or a recording of your voice to unlock your Android phone. The level of security vs convenience is not something I can decide for you. You'll need to evaluate that for yourself. But it is better to use Smart Lock than to use no lock at all!

- Fingerprint Unlock
  - o Using your fingerprint to unlock your phone is very common. Again, this is security vs. convenience. Your fingerprint is all over your phone and anything you touch so a hacker could lift and forge it. Also, fingerprints can be forged from photos of your finger.
- I should note that in the United States there have been cases where law enforcement has been able to force people to unlock a device via location or fingerprint (something you have) but may not be able to legally force you to enter a password (something you know). I am not a lawyer and laws and practices will vary by state and country. But it is generally understood that a password and only a password on your phone is the more secure method of protection of your privacy.

Setup Remote Wipe on your Phone

If your phone is connected to Google, iCloud, Office365, or Exchange you should be able to remote wipe it if you ever lose your phone.

Get notified whenever your data has been breached

 Sign up for https://haveibeenpwned.com/ -- this website monitors your email address (organizations can also monitor all email addresses on their domain name) for any data compromises or breaches associated with your email account.

Use Multifactor Authentication

Enable Multifactor Authentication on all important accounts. Your LastPass and Email account are important by default. You may also want to consider enabling MFA on your banking and retirement accounts and any account that would be catastrophic in case of a compromise.

Only buy Business Class Laptops

Stick to only the Business Class line of laptops from Dell (Latitude, Precision, XPS), Lenovo (Thinkpad), HP (Elite, ZBook, ProBook), Apple, or Microsoft. Consumer class laptops often come bundled with malware or adware software that can compromise security. Business Class laptops should include a TPM device that can be used for encrypting your hard drive. Always make sure your laptop comes with Windows 10 Pro (or Enterprise).

Encrypt Your OS Hard Drive

For Windows enable Bitlocker for your hard drive (requires TPM) and for Macs enable FileVault. This way if your computer is ever lost or stolen at least the data is encrypted.

Encrypt your Phone

Most Android and iOS devices have the ability to encrypt all your data. Many of them do this by default. Make sure this is enabled so that if your device is lost, as long as the screen is locked it will be difficult for hackers to get access to your data.

Don't Install Untrusted Software

The software you install on your computer should be from trusted sources. Often insecure websites with lesser known software can get infected with Malware. If it's widely used software from the official site, chances are it's okay. I have a rule that I will not install software on my computer even from a customer or vendor. If they absolutely need to install something, I'll setup a virtual machine and install it there.

Don't browse around a lot of sites, don't click on every link you see

Try not to browse around randomly and click things if you don't know what they are. Hover over a link to verify where it is taking you before you click. The more you stick to major trusted websites the less likely a malware-infection will take advantage of zero-day exploit on your browser.

Make sure website URLs start with https

HTTP is insecure. HTTPS / TLS is secure. Make sure your browser does not display a yellow or red warning. If a website is only http then don't send any financial data over it.

Use a DNS Filtering Service

Use a DNS Filtering service such as https://www.opendns.com/ or https://cleanbrowsing.org/ These services block known malware, ransomware, and infected sites at the DNS level which will help prevent your browser from being hijacked. Normally this would be setup on your home network's router, but if you frequently use your computer or phone on the road you can set it up for those as well.

Use the default Antivirus software that comes with Windows

The default Antivirus that comes with Windows is good. Third party antivirus software is often less secure. Just don't turn off the default Antivirus. On multiple occasions I've seen enterprises buy third party anti-virus software that they think is better only to find that they forgot to renew the licensing and nobody's antivirus was being kept up to date!

Use the Windows Firewall

The default Firewall for Windows is good. Just don't turn it off.

Be Mindful of Impersonations / Phishing Attempts

Be mindful of hackers impersonating your friends and coworkers. If you see a request to wire-transfer from the CEO be very careful. If someone calls you and needs something, make sure you verify it first. Many hackers will spoof an authority (someone high up in your company) and urgency (our vendor needs to be paid now or we'll miss the order) to trick people into doing things.

Don't Pick up Scam Calls / Respond to Scam SMS

Be discerning about calls from the IRS, Police, etc. I get so many scam calls that nowa-days as a general rule I do not answer my phone unless I recognize the number or am expecting a call. If it is that important, they will leave a message.

I also get a fair number of scam SMS messages. In both cases don't click on the links or respond. Block their number.

Do not Click on Links in emails to login to a website

If your bank sends you an email with a link; Don't click on it! Just go to your bank's website directly.

Do not load images on emails you receive unless you trust the sender

Those images almost always include tracking data and can even reveal your location.

Don't hook your contact lists up to other services

Don't allow LinkedIn, Facebook, etc. to have access to your contacts list. That's very rude to your contacts, and you can easily grant more access than they need.

Don't login with your Google or Facebook account on third party websites

It's so easy to do this… but it's more secure just to create an account with your email and password the old-fashioned way.

Pay Attention to Access Requests from Apps

If you download an App from the App store and it needs access to your storage, location, the microphone, or camera but you can't think of a reason it needs that, deny the access and uninstall the app. In most cases you can find another app or use the website.

Do not send sensitive data via Email

It's far better to use LastPass if sending passwords. Whenever you send an email be very careful about who you are sending it to and verify the attachments you are sending. I have seen many times where sensitive data is unintentionally sent in the clear to unintended recipients.

Use Individual Login Accounts When Possible

This is more for businesses and organizations, but if you have 2 or more people accessing a service, it is bad practice to share the same login. Instead create an account for each person and grant them the proper rights. That way when a person leaves the company you just disable their account. You're not having to reset all the passwords (which, let's be honest, you're not going to take the time necessary to do that).

Secure Your Wireless Network

Make sure your password is secure and your router is receiving regular security updates.

Setup a separate Guest Wireless network if you are able. This will prevent guests with infected devices from infecting anything on your home network. Get a cheap black and white laser printer to put in your guest bedroom and put it on the Guest Wi-Fi. AmpliFi sells home wireless routers that automatically keep themselves up to date with the latest security updates.

Don't Blend Your Work and Personal Devices

Don't use your work provided laptop or phone for personal use. Most organizations have full remote Administrator access to your work devices… they can install certificate authorities and push out software to your laptop at will. This means you can't trust those devices for personal use. You just can't. It is best to have separate devices.

Don't Use the Same Password for Multiple Sites

I often run across people that use the same password for more than one site. Don't do that! The reason is if your password gets compromised at any one site, a hacker can try that password against every major website and bank on the internet.

Appendix F: Free Authenticator Apps

The most popular Authenticator Apps for your phone are **Google Authenticator, LastPass Authenticator, Microsoft Authenticator**, and **YubiKey Authenticator** (if you have a YubiKey).

- **Google Authenticator** is very popular but it's the one I found the most lacking. Most authenticators have 2 fields per entry which makes it easier to store auth codes for multiple accounts against the same service. Google does not have this. Also, Google does not have an option to back up to the cloud. This could be more secure, but I think most users want their 2FA codes backed up. That said, Google Authenticator is not bad. But it is lagging the competition.

- **YubiKey Authenticator** requires a hardware token so I wouldn't recommend it for most people unless you're on the tech savvy side. The reason I prefer using it over an Android or iOS app is sometimes I need to enter in auth codes while I'm talking on the phone, a YubiKey doesn't require a phone, it can be inserted into a computer's USB port and authenticate that way. The YubiKey Authenticator is the only one with search capability. I have 2FA setup on a lot of services, so the search is nice. The downside to storing the codes in physical hardware is if you lose that YubiKey you've lost all your codes. There is no backup.

- **The LastPass Authenticator** is the option I think most people would use the most. 2FA codes can be backed up (handy if you lose your phone) and you get push notification for LastPass authentication.

- **Microsoft Authenticator** is another authenticator and works well especially if you use Microsoft services since it can do push authentication with those. Like LastPass it allows you to backup 2FA codes. Like the LastPass Authenticator 2FA codes can be backed up to Microsoft.

Appendix G: Is Some Vault Data Unencrypted?

A number of people, including security professionals, tell me that the LastPass Vault is an encrypted blob. This is not true. LastPass does not encrypt the entire Vault, but rather encrypts certain data within the vault. It is more accurate to say the sensitive data in the vault is encrypted. There are certain things that remain unencrypted.

This is the data in the Vault that is not Encrypted.

- URL field.
- Attributes and metadata such as autologin, is it a favorite, item type (is it a database, password, secure note), when was the last time it was accessed, etc.

Data in the Vault that is Encrypted:

- Name
- Folder
- Notes
- Username
- Password
- File Attachments
- Custom Field Data

Additionally, History and Account Settings (e.g. Country Restrictions) are obviously not encrypted.

Thanks

Well, now you know about everything I know about LastPass.

I hope you have enjoyed this guide over a nice cup of coffee.

Now you should know a little more about LastPass than you did before and I hope your time reading this was well worth it! **Thank you** for buying my first book! Maybe I will use the money to take my wife Kris out on a date tonight!

I'd like to thank my Dell Latitude E5450 laptop. Several times it got so far behind my typing or edits I thought it was going to give up and crash, but it hung in there and got the job done.

I'd also like to thank all the **people** who helped. I discussed just about every idea with Kris and she also made sure I had one night to myself each week to work on this. My son Eli helped me do a little proof-reading. In addition, Noelle Bryan (my sister) and Jeff Yesensky offered a ton of feedback, I bounced a lot of questions off them. Holmes Bryan (my dad) and Gregory Miller reviewed and corrected many grammar and style issues. And nearly all my family and friends helped in one way or another: reviewing landing page copy, making test purchases, tax advice, etc.

Made in the USA
Las Vegas, NV
29 July 2022